W9-CLK-938

THE ROMANTIC WORLD
OF MUSIC

ADELINA PATTI

THE ROMANTIC WORLD
OF MUSIC

BY

WILLIAM ARMSTRONG

Essay Index Reprint Series

 BOOKS FOR LIBRARIES PRESS
FREEPORT, NEW YORK

First Published 1922
Reprinted 1969

STANDARD BOOK NUMBER:
8369-1271-3

LIBRARY OF CONGRESS CATALOG CARD NUMBER:
71-90602

PRINTED IN THE UNITED STATES OF AMERICA

TO MY DEAR

Sarah Whitaker Glass

OF WEST VIRGINIA

CONTENTS

vii

ILLUSTRATIONS

THE ROMANTIC WORLD
OF MUSIC

THE ROMANTIC WORLD OF MUSIC

CHAPTER I

ADELINA PATTI

THE glory of Madame Patti's singing romance extended like a continued story from generation to generation. To turn to its beginnings is to dip into a long-gone past, for her début in opera was made at the Academy of Music, New York, in 1859; as a child she had concertized some years prior to that; her London début came in 1861; as the Marquise de Caux, she figured at the court of Napoleon III.

Yet at the age of fifty-two, after thirty-six years in opera, Madame Patti told of unbroken triumphs in this letter which she wrote to me from Hôtel du Luxembourg, Nice, on February 21, 1895:

I think when I wrote to you last I promised to send you news of my movements abroad. And you see I am faithfully keeping my word, which I can assure you is exceedingly difficult just now, as I am so busy that letter writing is almost an impossibility. We left the castle (Craig-y-Nos) about the middle of January, as I had to fulfill a concert engagement in Germany and Austria, before coming to Nice to sing in opera.

The success of my concerts was unparalleled, and in Berlin, Vienna, and Dresden the enthusiasm of the audiences was so great that I was in danger of being torn to pieces in their frantic endeavors to get on the platform to kiss my hands and my dress! It was exceedingly flattering to me and a little overpowering.

In Dresden the Crown Princess of Saxony was present, and expressed a wish to be presented to me, so amidst a scene of the wildest excitement on the part of the audience, who stood up and cheered without ceasing, I had to go to the Princess in the hall among the people, where she spoke to me for a long time and complimented me very warmly on my singing.

Since we came to Nice, about three weeks ago, our time has been almost entirely taken up in accepting invitations to lunch and dinners, invitations which pour in daily like the visitors, who come from early in the morning until late at night!

Last week I sang *Traviata*, when I had the most brilliant success imaginable. All my pieces were encored, and I had a perfect ovation at the end of the first act. The house was crammed from ceiling to floor, and the enthusiasm and delight of the audience increased from the beginning till the end until it knew no bounds, and in answer to innumerable recalls I was obliged to appear again and again. My entrée in the *Barber* was another succés fou. This week I sang *Lucia* and after that *Romeo.* . . .

Now I fear I must draw this long letter to a close, as we are dining at Beaulieu with the Grand Duke and Duchess Eugène de Leuchtenberg and I must go and dress.

Madame Patti's motto, which helped to keep her singing for so many years after this, was, "Who goes slowly goes safely." As she naïvely told me, "If I did not feel well, I did not sing, but went to bed and said there was no one in. The opera house might remain closed, but if there had been opera then, there would be no opera now."

King William I of Prussia, afterward German Emperor, made great preparations for a concert in which Patti, then in Berlin, was to sing. Not feeling quite well on the morning of a day that his Majesty had planned to be eventful, she made up her mind to stay in bed. To Meyerbeer, the composer of *Prophète* and *Huguenots*, was deputed the pleasant task of telling the Kaiser's grandfather that there would be no concert.

Madame Patti may or may not have considered the consequences. Of that she said nothing in telling this story, adding casually, "But the king did not resent it, for he came to hear me the next night I sang. 'Miss Patti,' he asked, 'what made you so ill?'

"'Your royal climate, your Majesty,' I answered." One can imagine the suspicious tone in which he uttered those words, "*so* ill," when almost overnight she appeared before him radiant and in fine voice. One can also imagine the royal good humor into which her quick retort put him, together with the winning smile and sly glance upward that, of course, went with it.

There were other reasons, very solid ones, why Madame Patti preserved her voice through growing years. Little Bauermeister, who sang long and valiantly at the Metropolitan, told me one of them. In ensembles at the end of an act, when chorus and orchestra were crashing at once, Madame Patti did not sing the prima donna's top notes. At Covent Garden it was always the good Bauermeister's mission to sing those top notes instead, and audiences were none the wiser.

The most important reason of them all, though, Madame Patti told me when we were doing an article together. It was this: "The middle voice is the one that you need to sing with. The gymnastics are very beautiful, but lose the middle notes and you lose all. Without the beautiful middle tones there is no *cantabile*, and upon the proper development of these, and the avoidance of strain by forcing of high and low notes the enduring power of the singer depends. The very high and very low notes are ornaments, but what good are Gobelins and pictures if you have no house to hang them in?

The true secret of preserving the voice is not to force it and not to sing when you ought not."

Madame Patti had the gift of repartee, and she had a very individual way in saying things that gave them added charm. On the morning after she had sung in a *soirée* at Baron de Rothschild's in London, I went to say good-bye to her at the Great Western Hotel, Paddington. Looking as fresh as possible, she was putting on her gloves to leave when I got there. "I didn't get home until four o'clock this morning," she announced gaily, "and I said to Carolina, 'Look at the sun! It's too early to go to bed.'"

Again, we were walking in the soft May sunshine on the terrace at her castle, Craig-y-Nos, in Wales. Patti's husband, Nicolini, then in his last illness, was being wheeled about in a chair. At every turn he managed that he met her. In his hands were catalogues of guns and fishing tackle. "Just to think of all those fish and I can't go fishing!" he exclaimed, "and all those ducks and I can't go shooting!"

"Never mind, dear," was her quick reply, "they will all wait for you." And the tone in which she said it, the enchanting flirt that she gave to her white parasol, made even the dying man grin.

It was in Chicago and in 1893 that I first met Madame Patti. Marcus Mayer was then directing what proved to be her last successful tour here.

Arditi of *Il Bacio* fame conducted the orchestra. Madame Arditi was along. Her hair, of the ghastly blackness that they keep in bottles in the Rue Cambon, was worn in elaborately plastered ringlets. It took so long to make them that when the train was due to arrive at their destination early, she would not let the sleeping-berths be made up at all. So poor Arditi had to sit bolt upright the night through.

On her arrival in Chicago, Mr. Mayer took me to call upon the diva. It happened to be the afternoon of a day in which she had read that she did not know how to sing the words of *Home, Sweet Home.* She was excited. Carolina Bauermeister, not the little Bauermeister of top-note fame, but the singer's companion for untold years, had used her eminent talent for promoting a disturbance. Arriving at Madame Patti's bed-side, she had broken the news by saying, "Good morning, Madame. You do not know how to sing *Home, Sweet Home.*" Then she produced the newspaper. That had taken place at nine o'clock in the morning. When I arrived at five P.M., Carolina's kindness was still actively working.

After the situation had been rehearsed in all its phases, Madame Patti said, "I am going to sing *Home, Sweet Home.* Tell me what is wrong with it?" Standing in the middle of the floor she gave the song from start to finish, making me stand beside her and follow the newspaper's account of her sung words. She held the music. I was expected to follow on that too. If my attention strayed, she would stop, reprove me, and begin afresh. When at last she had finished, she asked with a child's eagerness, "How else could I do it?" There was no assumption of arrogance or injured dignity, only desire to discover if she sang the words correctly.

In that song I have never heard any approach the beauty of Patti's *mezza voce*, gentle as a breath; the entrancing sweetness and the varied tone color of her voice carried clearly to the farthest limits of a vast hall. People, held spellbound, would bend forward in breathless stillness as if fearful of losing a single note, and when she ended a long sigh preceded the frantic outburst of applause.

Her singing of that same *Home, Sweet Home*, which a doubting Thomas had made Madame Patti herself doubt for a day, played a great part in her adventures. Of these she told me long afterward. One happened at New Orleans. In the middle of the performance, the gallery, which was filled to suffocation, started to sink. A stampede would have brought it down and caused a massacre. Foreseeing this, Madame Patti instantly began to sing *Home, Sweet Home*, without accompaniment, for the frightened orchestra had stopped playing. Sight of her standing there so calm, and sound of her entrancing tones in the dear, familiar measures not only reassured but charmed the audience into stillness. In describing the scene she explained simply, "It seemed the only thing for me to do."

Something similar happened at Bucharest. To get a look at her, a man had climbed high up on irons at the side of the stage; slipping, he fell on a woman standing in the wings. Badly injured, her cries rang through the theatre. Someone called "Fire!" In an instant the excitable audience was in a tumult. "It is no fire!" cried Madame Patti, and, as at New Orleans, started to sing *Home, Sweet Home*. In that frightened throng perhaps a handful understood the words she sang to them without accompaniment, but the sheer beauty of her voice brought calm and silence before she had ended the first verse.

It is curious, with this proven knowledge of her powers in singing *Home, Sweet Home*, that the diva should have given thought to the carping newspaper notice. Many great artists, however, suffer more acutely from petty faultfinding than from any other kind. Madame Melba in the height of her successes told me that she dared not read a New York newspaper for fear of seeing little, nettling personalities which would have made it impossible for her to sing at all.

Of courage Madame Patti had her share. She

was small, slight of build, with the traits of femininity demanded in Victorian days. But she was also a true child of the theatre. "If I am left alone," as she tersely put it, "I can always face a situation."

She herself told me an adventure of her début night, which came on Thanksgiving Day in 1859, when she sang *Lucia*, with Brignoli as *Edgardo*. A man had hung his coat over the gallery rail. In his pocket he had carelessly left a loaded revolver. It went off during the performance. Although Patti at the time was only sixteen years old, and that appearance was her first in opera, in relating her impressions of it she ended casually, "For an instant everyone on the stage stopped still; then we went ahead again."

The most exciting scene of them all came at San Francisco. "There," as Madame Patti described it, "I made my narrowest escape on the night a man threw a bomb on the stage. I had answered two recalls, entering from the center to make my acknowledgments. When I started out a third time, Carolina said, 'Don't go from the center, go from the wings. It will be a change.' I followed her advice. If I had not, I might have been killed.

"In the moment that I appeared for the third recall, the man threw the bomb. He had intended to fling it into a box occupied by a banker. Possibly from nervousness his aim proved bad. It landed in the center of the stage, just where I had intended to enter. The scene was indescribable.

" 'You might have killed Madame Patti!' I heard someone shriek as I stood there with a mouthful of smoke.

" 'I would have been glad,' he yelled back. 'She makes too much money as it is.'

"When things were quieted," Madame Patti added, "the opera went on, and I felt no bad effects. But then I am not hysterical."

The time that Jean de Reszke planted his heel on her foot in *Romeo and Juliet* at the Paris Opéra seemed to have left a more disagreeable memory with her than did fires and bombs. Late in life the two great singers became amicable toward one another, but that incident delayed their friendship until it was almost posthumous.

"Before he sang *Romeo* with me, when I created *Juliet* at the Paris Opéra," she told me, and her irritation grew with the telling, "he had sung every night, but nobody knew anything about him. When he could not get his high note, which was generally, he would plant his foot on the stage and strike an attitude. Of course no high note came, but he looked like it. Having his usual little trouble one night, he planted his heel with a thud in the middle of my slippered foot. De Reszke stopped to beg my pardon, and I stopped to tell him what I thought. Then we went on singing."

The threads of fate make strange weavings. Those same early performances of *Romeo and Juliet* at the Paris Opéra brought Madame Eames as well as Jean de Reszke to the Metropolitan. She followed Madame Patti as *Juliet;* Gounod, to whom Madame Marchesi, her teacher, took her, training Eames for the part. Her voice and her beauty did the rest.

There were moments when Madame Patti's iron nerve on the stage failed her when away from it. One night during my first stay at Craig-y-Nos, early in Nicolini's fatal illness, she came hurrying into the billiard-room nervously unstrung. "Something awful has happened!" she exclaimed. "Just now Nicolini staggered into my room holding onto the furniture. I started to catch him, for I feared he would fall. 'It is death! It is death!' he gasped. 'I know it is death.' I tried to soothe him. But I, too, thought it death. I tell you, these scenes are frightful: and there are so many of them now."

Just then, to give a nice little musical touch to the situation, that horrible orchestrion which she had in her billiard-room started playing Saint-Saëns' *Danse Macabre* with its rattling skeletons dancing on tombstones. And in rattling skeletons that orchestrion surpassed any orchestra. Nicolini had sent down a program to be played, and the cheery number led it off.

Whether all this was premeditated on the part of Nicolini, or was merely temperamental, I do not know. At any rate, he was ill for a long, long time after that before he did die. And always he insisted that Madame Patti sit by the hour in his room, while he feasted his eyes on her, seldom speaking.

I scarcely think, though, he held her love at that time; a situation which made her constancy all the more creditable. When I went in the early summer of that year to say good-bye to her, I spoke of her biography, which she had expressed the wish to do with me. "Come back next summer," was the reply, "and we will write it. Then *this* will be over, one way or the other." "This" meant Mr. Nicolini's illness, and her tone was quite serene in saying it.

Madame Patti had bought Craig-y-Nos because Nicolini loved the country. Fond of hunting and fishing, he would leave her alone for weeks at a time, while he enjoyed them on distant estates. Falling ill, he could not bear her from his sight.

Just how far she sacrificed herself to his wishes, she showed in the contents of this letter dated Craig-y-Nos, August 21, 1897, some months after the biography episode, and with Nicolini still lingering on:

I have been passing through a terrible time of anxiety and worry on account of Mr. Nicolini, who, about two months ago, had a very serious relapse.

As soon as he became a little stronger, the Doctors ordered him to Langland Bay, near Swansea, in hopes that he would derive benefit from the sea air. Unfortunately it makes me ill to stay near the sea, so for the last seven weeks I have been going backwards and forwards from the castle to Langland Bay to see him, leaving here at eight-thirty in the morning, and arriving at nine in the evening.

Mr. Nicolini, I am glad to say, is decidedly better for his stay near the sea, but last week he fancied the air was too relaxing and expressed a great wish to go to Brighton. We therefore arranged to have a comfortable invalid carriage for him, and he went to London on Tuesday last and is now at Brighton.

Next week I am going to London so as to be able to run down every day to see him at Brighton. . . . Of course my plans are very uncertain for the winter, as they must depend entirely upon the state of Mr. Nicolini's health."

There succeeded a long list of engagements proffered, to be accepted "all going well."

The following spring, Nicolini having finally departed some months previous, I got a letter from Madame Patti saying that she had had an arbor built below the castle terrace; that about it were planted full grown roses and clematis, and that she hoped to sit soon under their blossoms. She did.

With Baron Rolf Cederström, whom the next January she married.

So the biography was never done. Her explanation was that too many people's feelings would be hurt should it be written. Perhaps the real reason, though, was one on which she had remained silent. Her memories extended very far back indeed; Cederström was many years her junior.

Madame Patti's first marriage with the Marquis de Caux, equerry to Empress Eugénie, held doubtless a certain glamour of position for her. The devotion of de Caux was probably genuine, for she had then but a very small portion of the money which she eventually accumulated. Her first real passion, however, seems to have been inspired by Nicolini. She had then grown to womanhood, knew her own mind, and knew what love really meant. Temperamentally she risked the wrecking of her whole career to elope with him from de Caux.

Left to herself, this very odd romance would have never happened. Madame Patti always appeared to me as one prone docilely to remain in a rut once she was put there. According to an authority apparently reliable, Nicolini's part in the affair was the active one. Persistently he thrust his admiration on her; she as persistently ignored him. "That horrid man," was then her term in describing him. Undaunted, he made constant opportunity to meet her; once, according to this same source of information, concealing himself in a huge wardrobe in her bedroom, to appear suddenly before her.

At that time Nicolini was married and the father of many children; some who had heard him sing, have told me first of his tremolo and afterward of his tenor voice; to women who admired a large nose and slightly popped, but very amorous eyes, he must still have been regarded as handsome, even in his later life when I first met him.

At any rate, he won his aims completely. De Caux appears to have been well informed on the situation. In the midst of things, when Madame Patti was engaged to sing at the St. Petersburg Opera, the Marquis stipulated that Nicolini should be given no contract there. But he appeared on the scene, offered his services for nothing, and sang with Patti. De Caux arrived, making a violent disturbance; immediately Patti eloped to Italy with Nicolini.

Later on she bought Craig-y-Nos, and they made their home there. When, finally, a new divorce law was passed in France, they were married. His eldest son used to come over from France to visit at the castle. He called Madame Patti "mama." It was said in London at the time of Nicolini's death that in his will he had left Craig-y-Nos castle to this son, not expecting to depart before the diva.

For the conventional year, Madame Patti supported widowhood, having become engaged to Baron Cederström quite early in it. Meanwhile, the letter paper on which she wrote to me was so deeply bordered with black that there was slight room for words. Always Madame Patti had strict regard for the conventions set in her day by Victorian traditions; only once, through her love-affair with Nicolini, did she overstep the bounds of them. And even then, not willfully of her own seeking.

But that vividly romantic episode of her life proved beyond all contradiction that she had temperament sufficient to risk the greatest singing career then existing to be beside the one man she loved. And willingly the world forgave her, holding her as dearly as ever in its heart. With a voice as phenomenal as hers, that was a foregone conclusion.

Madame Patti felt things and felt them deeply. But emotion of the stronger kind was beyond her powers of expression in acting. Of this response in feeling, without the ability to express it, she gave clear evidence in a one-act opera written for her American tour of 1893-94. The music was too bad to deserve other than uncertain memory; I think, however, the piece was called *Gwendoline*. Its libretto, though, was not lacking in pathos of the old-fashioned sort, and this pathos Madame Patti plainly felt. With pained, strained expression on her face, and with clenched fists in trying climaxes she stood about on the stage; beyond this, nothing denoting feeling was conveyed in her portrayal.

To *Rosina* in the *Barber* and delightful kindred rôles in the lighter vein, Madame Patti brought the charm of her gaiety, her coquetry, and her distinction. Older opera goers declare her appearances as *Carmen* and as *Aïda* to have been unfortunate. Doubtless realizing that her limitations denied them to her, she promptly dropped the rôles. These episodes need not be dwelt upon. The diva gave us far too much to be thankful for and to eternally remember to allow of that. Her glorious singing in the old Italian repertory made her audiences forget all else. Patti's supreme vocal beauty in sustained melodies I have never heard approached. In her runs and florid passages, each tone was of an individual color, just as a great violinist gives a *cadenza* on his instrument.

And still, although she reigned preeminent throughout the world for so many years as singer of florid Italian music, she said this to me late in her career, and said it very earnestly: "I could not listen to *Traviata* and *Rigoletto* every night, even should Caruso sing them. But I never tire of Wagner's *Ring Niebelungen*. My voice was never the voice for the heavy Wagnerian things, but that does not prevent my devotion to them."

As a mimic Madame Patti was inimitable. An instance that I recall came in a story which she told once at dinner. It concerned Queen Victoria and two prima donnas whose lives had been filled with startling episodes. The first had sung in the royal presence, the ladies of her household being afraid to make disclosures.

When the second prima donna, however, was summoned to warble, they all braced up and poured some awful stories into the Queen's ear; finally becoming, indeed, so interested, that they thoughtlessly recited the entire histories of both.

It was at this horrifying climax that Madame Patti gave an imitation of Queen Victoria in excitement, her false teeth perilously slipping as she orated.

Madame Patti told this with the greatest gusto because, I think, she never really forgave the Queen for snubs put upon her on account of the Nicolini episode. It was not until long years after Patti had married him, and with flower-girls and other little proprieties, that Queen Victoria was prevailed upon to summon her to sing at Windsor Castle.

When, at last, the diva was invited, she had reached an age that made it necessary to ask her to stop there overnight, which was an exception to established custom. Dinner was served to her in her apartments, and, as a delicate attention, on silver plates. These scratched so at the contact of knife and fork that Patti could not eat, and went down famished to sing before the Queen.

Madame Patti's wedding with Baron Cederström was celebrated on January 25, 1899. She wrote to me from Rome one month later, told of Brecon *en fête* for the ceremony, at which Sir George Faudel Phillips gave her away, told of the guests present, and enclosed a menu of the wedding breakfast, served in a saloon train *en route* to London.

A second letter contained mention of a triumph she achieved while in the Eternal City and by her singing in concert before Queen Elena and the Italian court. Madame Patti was then fifty-seven. Should Pini-Corsi, the famous *buffo*, have been correct, she was three or four years older. He told me that his brother, who had sung with Patti in her early days, persisted in the statement that she was that much older than either her biographies recorded or she later acknowledged.

Baron Cederström, always quite frank regarding their disparity in ages, related an experience of his bearing on it. Soon after their marriage, the King of Sweden arrived in London. The Baron, accompanied by Madame Patti, called to register their names in the King's visiting book. Meeting the Chamberlain, Cederström asked, "Do you think his Majesty can arrange to receive my wife and myself later?" Word came back that the King wished, instead, to see them at once.

While Madame Patti was talking with Queen Sophie, the King, taking Cederström aside, asked in a whisper, "Are you happy?" Receiving an answer in the affirmative, he announced loudly, "I am glad." At that both Queen and diva stopped talking and were curious to know what pleasant news had brought the King relief.

In the autumn of 1900 Madame Patti visited Sweden, the native land of Baron Cederström, in company with her husband. On her return to Craig-y-Nos, she made mention of her reception in a letter dated November 12, 1900:

It was the first time I had been to Sweden, and our travelling through the country was quite a triumphal progress, for at every station we passed through, thousands of people came to welcome and cheer me, and in many places the police were obliged to keep order.

You have already heard of the charming way in which my husband and I were received by the King of Sweden, and of the beautiful order he presented to me, with signed photographs of himself and the Queen.

One afternoon at Craig-y-Nos, Madame Patti conducted me on a tour of inspection of her souvenirs. To see them was to feel the wonderful romance of her career. And the length of it! Kingdoms had changed to republics and wars wiped out boundaries, but the whole civilized world had continued to give her unswerving allegiance. On the floor of the drawing-room piled in one corner were silver laurel wreaths, so many in number that no place else could be found to put them; in cabinets were bon-bon boxes of every material, from simple mother-of-pearl to elaborately carved ones of gold, and out of every country; there were engraved gold invitation cards to dinners and banquets; a crown presented to her on the stage in South America; a wreath of laurel in gold, with the name of a rôle on each leaf, given her in Naples; there were caskets, one inlaid with silver and made of wood a thousand years old, part of a beam from the Priory at Brecon, and in which the freedom of the borough had been presented to her; there were lamps and other objects which had been buried under the dust of Pompeii until the day when she was carried through its ruins in a sedan chair and by special order all that was exhumed during her visit became her property.

In the library, where I cannot recall having seen any books, were illuminated parchments creating Madame Patti a member of musical societies in every part of the world, and there were intimate photographs of the kind that royalty reserves for its friends. Some of these looked like fashion plates of the early sixties. In her boudoir were fans given her and painted by Bonnaud and Lubarre, their sticks set with diamonds and rubies; a reproduction in gold, six inches high, of the great bell at Moscow; the chatelaine of Marie Antoinette; a silver drinking cup of Louis Philippe, and much more besides.

Several portraits of Madame Patti hung in the castle. The best one of these was placed in this same boudoir. It was by Winterhalter, who painted so many royalties and court beauties of the Victorian period. The most of his portraits are, of course, artificial, though of careful finish. But he might have been born a Moslem, for the women he depicted were not accredited with souls. This Winterhalter, however, presenting no deep complexities to picture in its subject, proved rather an exception. It represented Patti in the radiance of youth and joyful eagerness. The draperies were alive with motion.

That afternoon, while I was examining it, I heard a long-drawn sigh from Madame Patti, who stood beside me. Looking up I saw on her face an expression of infinite longing and regret. Instantly Madame Nordica's epigram flashed to mind: "A prima donna dies three deaths: When her beauty fades, when her voice fails, and when the breath leaves her."

And at that juncture I was glad that Carolina had left us; she would inevitably have invented a tactless speech. This she had done earlier in our tour. One of the boxes had disclosed a lost section of mother-of-pearl; a tiny, jeweled bird that should have chirped when meddled with had something wrong with its insides.

Madame Patti, evidently not given to dwelling among relics of her triumphs, exclaimed, "So much is wrong with things! I must get a man to mend them."

"Yes," assented Carolina, "they are getting old and dropping to pieces like we are."

Madame Patti, though her face expressed that she was furious, said nothing. But just then Carolina lost herself.

When the Patti Theatre, with its one hundred and twenty-six stage settings, was completed, Craig-y-Nos saw brilliant days. Eighty guests were entertained there for a week. Always a ducal style of living was maintained. These days had passed, however, before I met Madame Patti; mainly owing to Nicolini's ill-health. Nor were they resumed after her marriage with Baron Cederström. He, apparently, disliked her life-long friends and she was unlikely to fill the place with his own younger ones.

Prior to that, however, there was sustained as late as 1896 some of the accustomed and elaborate routine. After Madame Patti's return from America, the diva wrote to me of it in a letter dated August 31, 1894, saying:

We have given a great many plays and concerts in our little theatre. Amongst others, *Kathleen Mavourneen*, *Sonnambula*, *Fidelity*, and *Black Eye'd Susan*, of which I am enclosing you the programs.

Last week Lord and Lady Swansea visited us with a large party of friends, when we gave a performance of *Sonnambula*, which was preceded by a concert in which I sang Gounod's *Ave Maria*, Tosti's *Serenade*, and *Home*, *Sweet Home*.

On June 21, 1896, she wrote:

Later in the season the Prince and Princess of Monaco have promised to visit us, and amongst others we are expecting the Duchess of Leeds, the Marchioness of Blandford, the Ladies Churchill, Dowager Countess of Shrewsbury, and Sir Edward and Lady Swansea, etc.

Craig-y-Nos in its spaciousness was well fitted for entertaining. Built of stone, it stood in the heart of a great sweep of valley through which flowed a little river. On both sides rose mountains,

that one facing the castle being Craig-y-Nos or Rock
of Night from which the place took its name, and
where in the old days beacon fires of warning were
kindled.

A vast apartment roofed and faced with glass,
called the summer drawing-room, overlooked the
river and a great stretch of view. This led onto a
conservatory which held probably the first electric
fountain made; Nicolini bought it at a Paris exposi-
tion. Lighted at night, it was visible for twenty
miles.

Drawing-rooms, library, boudoir, billiard-room,
dining-room, theatre, and a great hall composed the
first floor; on the floors above were innumerable
suites and bedrooms, while in the wings were offices
and servants' quarters. Immense greenhouses, where
flowers, peaches and grapes were grown, stretched
in phalanx from one side of the castle. Running
the length of all was a broad terrace gently gradu-
ating to the river, and commanding a panorama of
the countryside. In the days of extensive entertaining, a retinue of sixty servants was required.

Madame Patti could sustain this outlay, her earnings in opera being, doubtless, the largest accruing
to any singer, and her active career the longest.
Caruso, for a limited number of performances, was
paid ten thousand dollars nightly. On the other
hand, Madame Patti told me of South American

engagements alone that she sang, each for a contract of sixty nights at six thousand dollars a performance.

Craig-y-Nos, its improvements, maintenance, and the lavish entertaining there, cost doubtless a great amount. Her earning powers had not continued throughout that period; this largely explains why the total fortune she bequeathed was about six hundred thousand dollars. When one considers, however, that Caruso's fortune, though far larger, came to a very considerable extent from royalties on his records, while Madame Patti's entire means were accumulated from actual singing before the public, her superior earning capacity in this direction would seem evident.

Shortly before she came to America for the last time in 1903, Madame Patti said to me, "It was my brother, Mr. Ettore Barili, who laid the foundation of my singing. My brother-in-law, Mr. Maurice Strakosch, taught me certain embellishments and *cadenzas;* but it was to Ettore Barili that I owed the foundation as well as the finish of my vocal training. With him I studied *solfeggii*, trills, scales; the chromatic scales came naturally to me."

Years later, I met in Paris Madame Amalia Strakosch, the widow of Maurice, and eldest sister of Adelina Patti. Madame Strakosch's version of Patti's training differed from the diva's. She told me, "My husband was Adelina's teacher, and her only one. He began to train her when she was thirteen; he taught her all her operas; for seven years he left me in America, because our children were too young to travel, and that he might devote himself to building up her career in Europe. I cannot understand why Adelina says that Ettore Barili was her teacher; he played her accompaniments sometimes, but my husband was the one who taught her all."

However these things may be, as far as they went with each individual instructor, I rather think that Madame Patti's voice was placed by nature, and that the most of her training came by intuition and the constant hearing of good singing. The big arias in the old operas she appears to have known and sung at an age when children are learning the alphabet.

Of those arias Madame Strakosch spoke that afternoon, and she recalled many other things that can awaken no controversy. Slight of figure, of medium height and elegant manner, she was the only one of the three sisters who had preferred home to the stage. "In *Norma*," she said, "my mother would sing the title part, my father *Pollio*, and I *Adelghisa*, and Adelina would appear as one of the infants.

"My mother had eight children by her two marriages; there were four Barilis; we three Patti girls, and our full brother Carlo, a violinist. What will the prima donnas of to-day say when I tell that our mother nursed every one of us?

"When the opera season was over, we would go from city to city in a stage, my mother, Adelina, and I, and give concerts. I remember one night when I had great applause, little Adelina's eyes shot fire. 'You think you are something,' she cried, 'but wait until they hear me!'"

The history of little Adelina was still very fresh in her mind: her varying moods; her constant presence in her mother's dressing-room, for she was too small to be left at home, and her singing even then of the big arias from the old repertory.

"The *Cavatina* from *Ernani* was a great favorite of hers," and Madame Strakosch, sitting there, began to sing its runs and roulades with a voice that was sister to Adelina's in color and facility. How old was Madame Strakosch then? She was singing *Azucena* in *Il Trovatore* when Adelina was seven, and her memories went back to the forties, and beyond them.

Had she not preferred home to the stage, she might have had a career almost equal to the diva's. Her voice was still lovely and her facility wonderful. "Don't tell," she said gaily, and her manner of saying things recalled Adelina's "but I am too lazy to practise." There you have it. She had doubtless not sung a *vocalise* for years, yet she had delivered the florid *Ernani Involami* with perfect ease. It was the Patti type of voice, and that incident seems but to confirm the opinion that nature was largely responsible for Adelina's training.

When I heard Carlotta Patti, I was a boy. If I can rely upon impressions made so early, I should say that her singing of the old arias was audacious in its assurance, and splendidly brilliant, but the tone quality was hard to the point of being metallic. However, I give this recollection for what it is worth.

Theodore Habelmann, the veteran tenor who sang the title part in *Lohengrin* in its New York production, told me this of the sad fate of Carlo: "Poor Carlo died in St. Louis while he was conducting the opera there, of which I was manager. One day I found him fatally ill at his hotel, where he had been excommunicated for not paying his bill. A thorough musician, he was never provident.

"Taking him to the little German place at which I stopped, I looked after him until the end. Then I telegraphed to Adelina and Carlotta Patti, telling them that their only brother was dead, and that two hundred dollars was needed to bury him. But I never received any answer from either one. At that time I had little money and, to save expense of a choir, we put the Latin words of the Mass to some of our opera numbers, and principals and chorus of the company sang at his funeral."

The grounds for this apparent cruelty I do not know. Madame Patti never mentioned to me the names of Carlotta, Amalia or Carlo. They were, doubtless, a temperamental family, which led inevitably to estrangements. The cause of that one arising between Madame Patti and Madame Strakosch I did hear, however. When the diva eloped with Nicolini, Maurice Strakosch followed her to Italy and went down on his knees begging her to leave the tenor. For this she never forgave her brother-in-law. That might have had something to do with her ascribing all credit to Barili as her teacher. Years after Strakosch's death, Adelina and Amalia were reconciled with many tears.

The final visit of Madame Patti to America made a tragic page in her singing romance. Some years previous to this, Mr. Loudon Charlton had asked me to speak to the diva of a tour here under his direction. I did, for her voice was then still beautiful. But she decided not to accept; her reasons I have forgotten. Had she come at that time the results would have been other. When, finally, she did reach here, a new generation had arisen. To it Patti was a stranger. She was then sixty-one years old. The selection as manager of Robert Grau, brother of the unforgettable Maurice Grau, of Metropolitan memory, promised disaster. Robert Grau was not able, or did not, at any rate, even forward passage money for Patti and her party. In the circumstances, why she relied sufficiently upon Robert Grau to come over for the tour, the diva alone knew. Madame Melba told me in London that Patti had promised Cederström the money brought by her American concerts. If Madame Melba's informant was correct, the situation explains much.

Late on a Saturday night she landed in New York. The Captain, it was of the *Etruria*, had gallantly promised to make port for Madame Patti on that day, no matter what the hour. Still fatigued from the voyage, she sang far from well the following Monday evening on her reappearance at Carnegie Hall. But in the succeeding concert, which took place the next Wednesday afternoon, she was completely rested, and almost the old Patti flashed forth. That was too late. Already the critics had written.

During the tour I had occasion to go to Philadelphia, where the day previous a disgraceful scene had transpired at the Academy of Music. Not enough tickets being sold for the Patti concert, it was postponed; failing to get their money back at the box-office, some started a riot.

Going to Madame Patti's hotel, I learned that she

was ill in bed, but saw Baron Cederström. When I expressed deep regret at the Academy of Music incident, he answered smilingly, "But *we* did not lose anything." That was his point of view; there was another.

In her wonderful day, Madame Patti had ruled the world; in her babyhood she was brought to America; in America she was reared; here she achieved her first and later a multitude of her greatest triumphs. Yet she had come home to have her named dragged into a sordid brawl at a theatre where not enough seats had been sold to guarantee her appearance. Somewhat later, when the engagement broke off abruptly, and Madame Patti came to New York to sail, she sent for me. She strove to hide the hurt, yet made it more apparent by constantly exclaiming, with forced gaiety, "Oh, I am so happy! To-morrow I am going home!" She was as a queen who had returned to her own country, where once all had worshipped her, only to find pitifully few subjects loyal.

Much of the old acclaim, however, was still remaining to her. The English, irrespective of age, have a gracious habit of growing old with their favorite artists. At Albert Hall the green-room was always packed during intermissions at Patti's concerts. Mingling with the younger element were stately dowagers and doughty old gentlemen. Those aged ones were her contemporaries and called her Adelina. Among them she appeared radiantly youthful by contrast. That is a blessed something which art does for those actively faithful up to the end. When, very late in her career, I spoke to Madame Patti of those intermissions and their assemblages, her eyes filled with tears as she answered, "It has been just the same since 1861."

Thirty-four years after that London début in 1861, and following a ten years' absence from the stage of the Royal Opera, Covent Garden, Madame Patti made her reappearance there, sustaining a series of the most glowing triumphs of her life.

That she felt very deeply the import of it all, is clearly shown in the following letter, the original of which is eight pages long, and which she wrote to me while her triumphs were still fresh in her mind, though I doubt if memories of those triumphs ever faded with her while life lasted. The letter is dated Craig-y-Nos Castle, July 10, 1895:

Now that I am back once more at dear Craig-y-Nos, and am able to find time to breathe again after the unceasing whirl of success and gaieties of the past four weeks in London, I devote some of my first spare moments to write and tell you about my season of triumphs. For it has indeed been one of the most gratifying triumphs of my career, to have returned to Covent Garden after an absence of ten years, and to have met with a reception, which I believe has never been equalled for enthusiasm, and to have repeated my successes of thirty years ago!

The house was a wonderful sight—it is said that not even on Gala Nights has such a display of royalties, notabilities, and diamonds been seen. Seats were at a premium, the stalls fetching ten pounds each.

The Prince and Princess of Wales with their daughter were present, also the Duke and Duchess of York, the Duchess of Fife, and the Duke and Duchess of Mecklenburg-Strelitz, and I was most warmly congratulated by the Prince of Wales on my success, and also on my return to Covent Garden. After the first act I had showers of bouquets, and the most beautiful baskets of flowers presented to me. Altogether it was a most memorable night.

The following Saturday I repeated *Traviata* with similar success—the Duchess of Coburg, the Crown Prince and Princess of Roumania, and the Grand Duke and Duchess of Hesse, etc., being present.

The *Barbier* was my next opera, and again the same story of a crowded house, masses of flowers, and another enormous success. I enclose you some articles which will give you a better description than I can of my performances, and will show you what the critics thought of me.

Don Giovanni drew a crowded house each time. In fact it was packed from ceiling to floor, the prices always being enormously raised. I finished my season last Friday in the *Barbier*, when I again received an unparalleled ovation. All the royalties were present. The Princess of Wales has been present on the occasions when I sang *Traviata*, the *Barbier* and *Don Giovanni*. Sir Augustus Harris was anxious that I should prolong my engagement, and sign again for next year, *"Mais, nous verrons!"*

Besides the opera I was invited to sing at the State concert at Buckingham Palace, the date of which was altered to suit my convenience. Last Wednesday I was present at a garden party at Clarence House, given by the Duke and Duchess of Coburg, when I was congratulated by all the royalties present on my recent success at Covent Garden. . . .

Quite aside from the honors that were shown her then and afterward in Great Britain and on the Continent, wherever and whenever she might sing, there was another phase of life that brought her joy. And that was the almost feudal loyalty displayed toward her by her humble neighbors. Always on her return to Craig-y-Nos, there was a scene of hearty welcome. In a letter that she wrote describing one home-coming she described all. It said: "I was immensely touched at the reception given me in the neighborhood, for when we went driving all the tenants of Swansea valley had erected flags and banners and stood in the roadside, some with tears in their eyes, to wave their hands and welcome me home."

All her life long she had been used to an homage more universal than that accorded sovereigns. True child of the theatre, she joyed in it, whether it came from the great world or was simply expressed by simple people. And it made a golden halo for her up to her golden end.

CHAPTER II

LILLIAN NORDICA

THE glamour of Madame Nordica's career was the greatest that has come to any American singer. In England she was as beloved as she was at home, for in England she had made a name in opera before we heard her at the Metropolitan.

Madame Nordica's London home in those days was Clarence House, on the borders of Regent's Park. There her staunch friend Sir Arthur Sullivan, then in the heyday of his popularity, was a frequent visitor, and with him came the Duke of Edinburgh, Queen Victoria's youngest son. King Edward VII, at that time Prince of Wales, learned to know her through this music-loving brother, and ever after kept in sympathetic touch with her career. Before Queen Victoria she sang both at Osborne House and Windsor Castle. Queen Alexandra, the Duke and Duchess of Connaught, the Duchess of Teck, Queen Mary's mother, and the Duchess of Manchester, mother of the present Duke, were among the steadfast friends her golden voice made for her.

In her girlhood in Boston, Lillian Norton, as she was then known, was employed in Sargent's book shop. At lunch time, having often no money to pay for the meal and too proud to let it be suspected, she would walk during that lunchless lunch hour and return to work at the end of it. Madame Nordica herself told me this, adding, "But don't say anything, for 'D' with his foreign ideas would not like it." "D" was Mr. Zoltan Döme, her second husband.

One Sunday in the Black Forest, when we were all out walking, and no busy people appeared in the landscape, he exclaimed, "How I hate Sunday! I like to see people at work." He never appeared to work himself. In the course of her earlier pronounced successes in Wagner, Madame Nordica said bluntly, "Plenty have voices equal to mine, plenty have talent equal to mine. But I have worked." Whatever she found to do, she did it unsparing of herself. I have known her to get out of a sick bed, go to the Metropolitan and sing, and then return to bed again. Doubtless her Puritan spirit supplied the motive power. Her father, Edward Norton, and her mother were both descended from Thomas Mayhew, Governor and owner of Martha's Vineyard and the outlying islands. Her mother, *née* Allen, was of the same stock as Ethan Allen of Revolutionary fame, and her family had intermarried with descendants of both Captain Miles Standish and of John Alden and Priscilla.

It was not until after the death of her next older daughter, who gave great promise as a singer, that Mrs. Norton centered her ambitions on the youngest child, Lillian, up to then overshadowed by her sister. Trained by John O'Neill of Boston, Lillian Norton got her first important engagement with Gilmore's band to tour this country, later going to Europe with the organization. And in Europe she remained to study repertory with San Giovanni at Milan, paying her expenses with money she had earned.

Her début was made at Brescia. There, a few nights later, she sang *Alice* in *Roberto il Diavolo*. That performance marked the first appearance of a little solo dancer in the elaborate ballet. As a wicked nun she had to rise on a trap from her grave at midnight, and dance in the moon-lit graveyard. Greatly excited, and decidedly nervous at thought of ascending on the trap, the little dancer stood shivering beneath the stage. Beside her was her mother, a weazened Italian, the inevitable black shawl over her head. Under one arm rested a long loaf of bread, under the other a gorgonzola cheese.

Seeing her daughter's fright, she jumped on the trap, exclaiming, "Who's afraid!" In that instant the trap shot upward and with it the old woman, bread, cheese and all. Her unexpected advent caused the audience to gasp, then roar with laughter. Even when, at last, things were quieted, if someone tittered at the recollection, hilarity burst forth again.

In Russia the real romance of Lillian Nordica's career started. There, following her Italian début, she sang in a company of which Madame Sembrich and Miss Clara Louise Kellogg were members. Young, beautiful, singing such rôles as *Cherubino* in *Nozze de Figaro*, and fêted by titled society, she was received at the court of Alexander II, then in brilliant days. The young Grand Dukes vied with each other for the honor of escorting her up a side stairway to great functions at the palace, and that she might escape the tedious delay of arriving with the court at the main entrance. Presently, all this was cut short by the Czar's assassination and the closing of the opera. Final days in St. Petersburg proved a nightmare; there was a house-to-house search, in which even the opera singers were not spared.

Going shortly on tour with some of the younger members of the company, she sang in concert at Danzig, being with her mother a guest of the Governor's wife. During her stay a meeting of the new Czar and the German Emperor William was planned to take place at the Governor's palace.

Every precaution was exercised to secure safety. The cellars were wired from end to end, and equipped with alarm bells, so that the royal party might not be blown into the air, or at least, not without warning. On the day set for the sovereigns' meeting, soldiers stood shoulder to shoulder from the palace to the quay. But the new Czar was afraid to come, remaining aboard his yacht in the outer harbor. Madame Nordica told me that she heard Bismarck exclaim on hearing this, "He *must* come!" On horseback the Iron Chancellor thundered out of the courtyard, followed by a retinue of officers. When he returned, the Czar was with him.

On the threshold of this life in which her youthful heart gloried, came a break. For two years she left the operatic stage. She had made her début at the Paris Opéra as *Ophelia* in Ambroise Thomas' *Hamlet* and sung out successfully the engagement, when she married Mr. Frederick Gower, an American. Her chief desire in making this marriage seems to have been to provide a home in which her mother might be sheltered. Mr. Gower required in return that Madame Nordica forsake the stage. Her share of the contract was held, his quickly broken.

On that which followed it is unnecessary to dwell at length. Madame Nordica pronounced him mad; his eccentricities could not well have been otherwise explained. Putting new garments on the open grate fire, he would gleefully watch them burn, meeting her remonstrance with, "*I* have paid for them." He also had a passion for burning her music, and in the presence of guests would insist on her singing the arias whose notes he had destroyed. In reality he hated to have her sing at all, often asserting, "If you only knew how like a monkey it made you look, you would never sing." After two years of this, she left him and proceeded to get a divorce.

The story of Mr. Gower's ascent at that juncture in a balloon, a storm brewing, and the subsequent discovery of its empty wreck floating in the English Channel, is well known. Then came Madame Nordica's return to opera in Great Britain. A prima donna who was in the company with her told me that often rumors came, sometimes printed ones, telling that Mr. Gower had been seen in India, in Russia or in some other country. These rumors threw Madame Nordica into a state of terror. One night, in her dressing-room at the theatre, she heard of Gower's presence in England. So frightened that she could not stand without support, she was led into the wings, and then, with that indomitable will of hers, went out and sang. Of course this rumor, like all the rest, was without foundation.

When the opera company with which Madame Nordica had been appearing in the British provinces arrived in London, the manager, Colonel Mapleson, was long in arrears with salaries. Of her début at Covent Garden as *Violetta*, she said to me, "I had not the money to pay for a cab that night, and walked to the theatre and back, with one flight of stairs beyond the elevator to climb after I reached the Charing Cross Hotel. In those days it was a question whether I should sup or whether I should dine. My mother was ill in Italy, and needed my help. I tell you, no one knows what I have suffered and what I have been through.

"When I came out on the stage that evening there stood a tenor as *Alfredo* whom I had never seen before. And such a tenor! Of course my ensemble numbers were ruined, but I had a chance in my arias, and how hard I tried in them. The next day I was known in London."

Years afterward Bernard Shaw told me that he remembered the night well, and that Madame Nordica had been given an *Alfredo* from the chorus, the regular tenor refusing to appear because Mapleson already owed him much and could pay nothing.

Among other memories of her upward swing in days that followed, Madame Nordica recalled a visit by the Duke of Edinburgh at Clarence House one hot afternoon. He was thirsty and asked for a glass of lemonade. She rang for her butler to bring it. They waited. The Duke's thirst grew, and with it Nordica's embarrassment. At last the door was flung wide and a procession of two entered. Both men bore silver trays aloft, as the Holy Grail is carried in *Parsifal.* On the one tray rested the Duke's lemonade, on the other a sugar bowl. Intuition flashed an explanation in the singer's mind. The butler, feeling a visit by his Queen's son to demand ceremony, had scoured the neighborhood for an extra man sometimes employed at Clarence House, and put him into clawhammer. When the door was closed on them Madame Nordica explained things, and the Duke roared at the joke.

Long afterward, and following Madame Nordica's appearance as *Elsa* in the first Bayreuth performance of *Lohengrin*, the Duke of Edinburgh, then the reigning Duke of Saxe-Coburg-Gotha, invited her to sing the rôle at his opera house. As special attention he ordered her dressing-room hung with roses suspended by threads from the ceiling. Of course, their suffocating perfume put her in bad voice. For all its charming thoughtfulness, royalty sometimes misdirects its kindness, as Madame Patti also found in her experience with the silver plates at Windsor Castle.

Madame Nordica I first met in 1893, and for twenty-one years, up until her death, we were friends. At the date named she was singing with the Abbey-Grau Company, and in days that were rightly called the golden ones of opera. Among her colleagues were Melba, Calvé, Eames, the de Reszkes, and Plançon; she sustained her place beside them brilliantly. At that period she was studying tremendously. Toiling would be a word better to describe it. She learned a rôle slowly and with infinite pains, but once learned it became fixed in mind indelibly.

Prior to preparing for her Bayreuth début, ner most arduous work was done in London, at the outset of her operatic life; one rôle after another she memorized with or without hope of singing it. Always when called upon she was ready to replace an absent prima donna. Her evolution from coloratura rôles to those of *mezzo carattere*, and finally big dramatic ones was made step by step, legitimately, logically.

We who heard her later, and only in heroic rôles, do not, perhaps, realize that she sang aside from *Violetta* and *Ophelia*, the *Lucia*, the *Queen of Night* in *Magic Flute*, the *Inez* in *L'Africaine*, the *Gilda* in *Rigoletto*, and an array of coloratura parts.

Only lately Madame Schumann-Heink said to me, "In the days of Nordica's singing of Italian and coloratura rôles, her velvety tones were better than those of any singer among them all. What a wonderful voice it was! When will there be such another? Her high C in Verdi's *Requiem*, spun out like a thread of golden light, was something that will linger in my memory eternally."

But it was the heroic Wagnerian rôles that brought to Madame Nordica her greatest glory; the *Brünnhildes* of the *Ring*, the *Kundry*, the *Isolde*. This last was, perhaps, her greatest achievement. In it her splendid trumpet tones, her tones of subdued, passionate tenderness were of supreme beauty, her action was alive with tragic intensity. A detail of it, minor, but eloquent, was the fluttering management of her draperies which I have never seen equalled save by Miss Ellen Terry.

Shortly after her first appearance in the part she wrote to me:

It would seem almost needless to say that I fully intend to continue my study of Wagner's heroines. It is with the keenest pleasure that I look forward to the three *Brünnhildes*. Already I am nearly finished with *Siegfried*. This summer I will study *Götterdämmerung*, and complete *Die Walküre*. I think the study of this music has been of great benefit to my voice and strength. I love it. *Isolde* is all to me.

With Jean de Reszke in the companion part, those performances at the Metropolitan of *Tristan und Isolde* became historical.

During Mr. Grau's régime, the music dramas began at seven-thirty. One *Tristan* night things went

LILLIAN NORDICA AS BRÜNNHILDE

wrong; Madame Nordica's maid had by mistake
brought her *Elsa* costumes instead of those of *Isölde*,
and had to return home to fetch them. Meanwhile,
terribly nervous, the singer paced her dressing-room.
At last she was ready, but the curtain was thirty
minutes late. Some meddler had told Mr. Grau
that Madame Nordica, disliking early presentations,
had willfully caused the delay. Going at once to
her on the stage just as she was posing herself on
the great white bearskin rug for the first act, he
began a tirade. "Leave my presence!" she cried,
"Leave my presence!" Suddenly grasping a fact
which she had fully realized, that a quarrel would
put her in bad voice for the whole performance, he
left abruptly.

Madame Nordica's *Aïda* was a superb creation,
as was her *Valentina* in *Huguenots*. Both must be
placed in the gallery of heroic portrayals that she
gave us. The *Valentina* she, herself, claimed as
vocally much more trying to the voice than any
Wagnerian part she had essayed, Meyerbeer having
written with far less vocal understanding than had
Wagner.

Many of us remember, too, her vivid *Leonora* in
Trovatore, her tragic *Donna Anna*, her *Kundry*, her
Venus in *Tannhäuser*, and her *Susanne* in *Nozze
de Figaro*. Those were the chief rôles, aside from
the Wagnerian heroic ones, and *Gioconda*, that

marked her later career. But the rôles that she had
learned and sung at one time or another numbered
thirty-two.

There is no doubt that Madame Nordica's studies
at Bayreuth under Madame Cosima Wagner proved
of tremendous value to her. Following her appearance as *Elsa* at the Bayreuth *Festspielhaus* began
the glorious climax of her singing life, for then all
that she had previously learned seemed to crystal-
lize.

Madame Wagner's ideas on training artists in
her husband's music dramas were by no means in-
fallible. She instilled, however, the utmost exact-
ness; self-subjection to the rôle, and elaboration of
detail. Above all, she aroused the imagination.
None whom I knew sang at Bayreuth without
merging the greater in artistic stature.

But there was an exaggerated ego affecting those
ideas of Madame Cosima which proved extremely
humorous. Madame Lili Lehmann caught the spirit
of this when she announced caustically, "Since
Cosima has written the operas I can no longer sing
them."

Madame Amalia Materna had, perhaps, the most
delicious and illuminating experience of them all.
She was Wagner's first *Brünnhilde;* he had trained
her in the part. Summoned to appear at Bayreuth,
Madame Wagner began to re-teach the veteran her

Brünnhilde. Immediately the two fell to quarrel-ling. And they kept it up. Materna, after she had grown hoarse from talking, remembered that which she might have said before, "The master, *himself*, taught me this rôle!"

"Never mind," swept back Madame Wagner, "poor Richard didn't always know himself what he wanted."

For all her ardent interest in her husband's noble music, and her accredited insight in imparting it, devotion to her son, Siegfried, seemed to make Ma-dame Wagner equally partial to his mediocre operas. Madame Destinova, or Emmy Destinn as we better know her, told me an incident shedding strange light on the situation.

Called to Bayreuth to sing *Senta* in *Fliegende Holländer*, she went on arrival to Villa Wahnfried. Madame Wagner, ill in bed, sent for the prima donna to come to her room. During the parley a piano began to tinkle. "Hush!" said Madame Wagner impressively. "My son's music." And sitting up in bed she listened in rapt ecstasy until the last in-nocuous note sounded.

Later, the two women quarrelled so energetically that even Siegfried's "music" might easily have es-caped attention, and in wrath Destinn forsook the little Franconian city.

Possibly there has been more quarrelling to the

square inch at Bayreuth than in any corresponding area on the earth's surface. That summer of the first *Festspielhaus* performances of *Lohengrin*, it reached carnival proportions. Popovici, the Rumanian baritone, and the greatest *Telramund* that I have seen, always answered Cosima's commands at rehearsal with a cheerful "Yes," sometimes following her directions, sometimes not. In the first public presentation of *Lohengrin*, and with her at safe distance, he did everything exactly his own way, firing the audience to wild enthusiasm. Though a blow to her authority as dictator, this was as nothing compared to a disturbing development shortly preceding it.

Madame Nordica had studied with lamblike docility under Cosima's tuition, and was letter-perfect in the *Elsa*. All Germany was in an awful uproar over the fact that a foreigner instead of a native had been chosen for the rôle. In the midst of it, Madame Nordica presented the little request that Zoltan Döme, with whom she was then deeply in love, should sing the title part in *Parsifal*. What Madame Cosima said is unknown to me. King Ludwig of Bavaria built Wagner's Villa Wahnfried solidly. Its walls withstood the shock.

When Madame Cosima's reply came, it was a most emphatic "No." Thereupon, Madame Nordica fainted. When she recovered, she asked weakly for a schedule of departing trains, and ordered her trunks packed, including the brand new one she had bought to hold *Elsa's* costumes.

Hearing the news promptly, for all news travels promptly at Bayreuth, Madame Cosima doubtless grasped the situation. At that late date, another *Elsa* could never be trained in her own ideas. Those first *Lohengrin* performances in Bayreuth's history were intended as the crowning episode of that year's festival. So Döme sang *Parsifal*—once. And Van Dyck, who regarded the part of *Parsifal* as having been written solely that he might sing it, paced up and down in full view of Döme while he wrestled with its measures on the stage.

That summer at Bayreuth things happened off the stage as well as on it. In the former episodes, Madame Lili Lehmann quite carried off the palm. Madame Wagner gave a reception at Wahnfried to all the singers. Madame Nordica, as a younger artist, and with sweet intentions toward the veteran Lili, asked, "May I come to see you, Madame Lehmann?"

Quick as a flash Madame Lehmann turned upon her and replied, "I am not taking any pupils this season." Needless to add she put her emphasis on the sixth word of the sentence. In that moment the buzzing of a fly would have been audible in Wahnfried's theatrical *grand salon*, for everyone who had not heard the speech felt that something horrible was in the air.

But all was later forgiven, and perhaps forgotten, by those two great women, who became measurably affable toward one another. One night they were appearing in an opera together. Madame Lehmann needed a pair of black silk stockings, her own having been left behind at the hotel. Madame Nordica happened to have an extra pair, and saved the situation.

Madame Lehmann returned them with this note: "Here are your stockings. I know they are clean because I washed them myself. I told your husband that I thought your voice improved. Now I hope you are satisfied."

Madame Cosima appeared to hold no grudge against Madame Nordica because of the fainting episode, perhaps remembering temperamental moments which she herself had in achieving Richard. Very soon she was training Madame Nordica, with Herr Kniese's help, in *Isolde* and the *Brünnhildes* of the *Ring*. The *Isolde* was imparted at Lucerne, where the only room in which such proceedings seemed quite welcome was above a hairdresser's shop and overlooking a stable yard. There were two chairs in the place. Herr Kniese, of necessity, used one at the piano, Madame Cosima sat on the other.

Some years later, Madame Nordica sang *Isolde*

at the Munich Festival; for that Madame Wagner never forgave her, Bayreuth and Munich being then at sword's points. Other prima donnas, however, flew to Munich on slight provocation, and returned absolutely without sackcloth to be welcomed at Bayreuth. But Madame Nordica was allowed no such privilege. The situation rather implied compliment.

Following this, Madame Nordica next cast her shadow in Bayreuth as a festival visitor the summer previous to Mr. Conried's production of *Parsifal* at the Metropolitan. As she was to sing the *Kundry* she wished to view the part in its performance. Her stay was in strong contrast to an earlier one in which she had been fêted. Madame Cosima showed not the slightest recognition of her presence. Presently she gave a luncheon at Wahnfried to all the artists visiting Bayreuth, Nordica alone being slighted. At that the great American vowed never to return, nor did she.

However, on the day of Madame Wagner's festivity, Madame Nordica also entertained. Her guests were the Duke and Duchess of Connaught, who lunched with her in the old garden of Hôtel Sonne; one of those German small town inns where the cooking is delightful and nice little piles of dust linger in the corners of the stairs.

At that time Madame Nordica had separated

finally from Döme. She wired me at Vienna to hurry on to Bayreuth if I wished to escort her back to Paris, which, of course, I did. With her was Madame Baskerville, who had coached Calvé and many another in their operatic rôles. Together we three spent happy afternoons in the garden at Rollwenzel, a little inn where dear Jean Paul Richter used to write all day, his wife sending the children across the fields from Bayreuth for him when he forgot to come home to supper.

The final afternoon of the festival Madame Baskerville started off to Nüremberg to engage rooms for our party, Madame Nordica following with me by a later train after the *Parsifal* performance. We got the last carriage in waiting at the theatre, and a drunken driver. Twice, by accident, his whiplash struck her across the face. Catching him by the collar, I threatened arrest. Then, in peace, we reached the railway station.

Madame Nordica, very nervous from the incident, started toward the restaurant, exclaiming, "I *must* smoke a cigarette." The place was crowded; everyone knew her by sight. Smoking, except by Russian women, was less common in public then than it is now.

"Let's smoke outside," I urged. Out we went. Around a dark corner of the building, I found a hand-truck. Perched on it we were smoking comfortably when I observed first one head, then another, thrust around the corner. Presently, I realized that in shielding her from one source of prattle I had led her into another even worse. But that time my persuasions that we move on were fruitless. And our spying audience continued.

Settling herself comfortably in the compartment on the train, Madame Nordica, with a blessed faculty she had in travelling, was soon asleep. Opposite her a man sat motionless, his eyes fixed on her face. Apparently the dream of his life was realized in seeing at close range one who had given him infinite artistic happiness. At Nüremberg I told her of it.

"Oh! did I snore?" she asked excitedly.

Little adventures on that little journey seemed not to end. Next morning early we were on the Nüremberg platform waiting for the Paris train. Eight minutes before it left Madame Nordica discovered a bag missing. It contained fifty thousand dollars' worth of jewelry. She remembered nothing about the appearance of the hotel porter who had taken it in charge. Frenzied search for a bag with a man began and ended unsuccessfully. As the train was about to move he hove in sight. There had been no scene, nor did Madame Nordica again allude to the matter.

At another time that same bag was misplaced for two days on shipboard between New York and Southampton. She was going to London for the season, and it contained one hundred thousand dollars' worth of jewels. To make matters worse, the lock was broken, and anyone could readily have opened it. After forty-eight hours the bag was found, intact, in a second cabin stateroom.

It has been said that the value of Madame Nordica's jewelry was four hundred thousand dollars. I remember a day when the late Duchess of Manchester came to the Hôtel Savoy in London to borrow a lot of it to wear at the costume ball given by the Duchess of Devonshire during Queen Victoria's Diamond Jubilee. But at the opening of the season 1903-04 Madame Nordica returned to New York from Europe minus the whole collection from diamond tiara down. To me her brief explanation was, " 'D' has kept my jewels in Paris to have them reset."

Madame Nordica and Mr. Döme were just then at the point of separation. French law made a wife's jewels her husband's property. Later, the collection reappeared in her possession, but that season, to avoid public comment on lack of any jewels at all, she had borrowed a diamond necklace from her cousin, Mrs. Stoiber, then resident in Paris.

A letter came to me regarding the necklace. It

was undated, but bore the postmark of April, 5, 1904, and was mailed on tour. At that time Madame Nordica had broken absolutely with Mr. Döme. She made brief allusion to this in her letter, which was as follows:

Thank you, dear friend, for your good letter. I am off—for another tour. Let me know your Paris address.

I am sending you a diamond necklace which belongs to my cousin Mrs. Stoiber, 92 Champs Élysées. Will you deliver it into her own hands and tell her I have written to her twice.

Please have it in a safe place—while travelling.

I am so sorry for "D"—but I can do nothing but go my way.

If it troubles you to take the necklace, you can leave it with Mrs. Walker—*

Thank you—and know that I am your friend—

L. NORDICA

The trust, I, of course, accepted, taking the necklace over with me when I sailed shortly afterward. During a month's stay in London I kept it at the bottom of my trunk, piously hoping that it would still be there when I looked for it, which was often.

Finally, with the necklace in my norfolk jacket pocket, sewn tightly shut, I crossed the channel on my mission. Somehow, the nearer I got to Paris,

---

* Mrs. George Walker, her sister, and then in New York.

the greater grew my anxiety, until, after a restless night, I deposited the diamond necklace on Mrs. Stoiber's breakfast table beside her morning coffee. The incident occurred some years later than that which immediately follows.

CHAPTER III

LILLIAN NORDICA

(*Continued*)

QUITE by accident, Madame Nordica heard of
Bad Boll in the Black Forest, and went there
to study the summer in which she sang *Tristan und
Isolde*, given without cuts at the Munich Festival.
This was the engagement which aroused Madame
Wagner's wrath.

As Madame Nordica had planned to do some literary work with me, I was of the party, which included Mrs. William Salomon, a charming, cultured woman and wife of the New York banker.
Together we three would take long walks. One day
our way led past a peasant's cottage, under whose
trees two little girls were cuddling bundles of rags
as dolls. The next afternoon Madame Nordica and
Mrs. Salomon took me for a longer tramp, ending
at the nearest village. There, in its sole toyshop,
the owner unpacked his entire Christmas stock. The
two best dolls were chosen, and we trudged back to
the peasant's home, reaching it at dusk. Already

the entire family was in bed. After long delay and much calling, a man's sleepy head appeared at an upper window. Presently, two little girls, barefooted and in their night clothes, were shrieking with delight as each held in her arms the first doll she had ever owned.

Always those little thoughtful acts were scattered through the summer days when it was my fortune to be with Madame Nordica. She picked up odd friendships with the simple folk about her, making their lives one with hers. Never knowing her real identity, they seemed to sense her greatness, but that grandly gracious air of hers won their ready friendship.

Bad Boll, lying in a deep, cuplike valley, lacked the vigorous air promised at Menschenschwand, a Black Forest resort eighteen miles distant. So presently our party journeyed there by primitive vehicles. Midway at a peasant's home we lunched. Madame Nordica donning an apron went into the kitchen and prepared a salad, while our hostess, unresentful and confiding, cooked a lovely *wiener schnitzel* to go with it.

At four o'clock each afternoon at Menschenschwand, Madame Nordica sang *Isolde's* music to us in the Hunter's Dining-room, its walls hung with trophies of the chase. Her voice in all its golden prime would float out into the garden, where bands of tourists tramping the Black Forest rested, listening in wonder to that great voice in that great music coming to them from a wayside inn.

It was a charming place, set between tall mountains, a little river chasing through the checkerboard of vari-colored fields that floored the valley. Sometimes in our walks along the hard, white highway leading to St. Blasien and thence to the big world far beyond, fawns would creep through the tall grain almost hiding them, to eye us curiously as we passed.

Two episodes made up the program of the local day. At five in the morning, often earlier, all the cows and goats, with their shepherds, marched in procession from the village to the mountain top which overlooked it. At six in the evening, all marched back, each beast dropping out in turn at the shed it knew by instinct. Then the day was done.

The inn itself stood perched against the lowest ledge of a spur of mountain, so that the third story in the front became the first story in the rear. That was why a cow, mistaking a back entrance to the inn for one opposite it, and leading to her stall, tumbled downstairs into the second story of the inn. She landed with a crash against the door of Romayne Simmons, Madame Nordica's accompanist. Peering out, a hot breath steamed in his face and two great eyes glared at him in the dusk. Thinking, quite excusably, that the devil had arrived, his cries set the place in an uproar.

Fads in singing Madame Nordica despised. That summer there came to us a baritone friend of Mr. Döme, and whose one thought centered in his diaphragm. In all his waking hours and likely in his sleep, it was eternally his diaphragm. Never then and never since has he sung the rôle of *Wotan*, but he owned the costume. One day he donned it, long cloak, big hat and all, to go with us on a picnic at the Bismarck monument which crowns the Black Forest.

Simmons, skylarking, slipped and fell on the ribs of *Wotan*, lying on the grass. Seeing the commotion, Madame Nordica hurried towards it, exclaiming to me dryly, "This time it *is* his diaphragm."

As we neared the group a disabled *Wotan* was being propped against a tree. When he got his breath his first words were, "But for my wonderful diaphragm, I'd have been killed."

The next summer at St. Moritz in the Engadine did not begin happily. Madame Nordica was utterly worn out from the Metropolitan season, a long concert tour, and twelve appearances in heroic rôles at Covent Garden, London. More than once during this last engagement she came dangerously

near to collapse. Sometimes fully dressed to start
to the opera or a social function, and unable to move
until forced to go, she would suddenly summon
every atom of reserve strength and become a trans-
formed, dominant being.

There was one pilgrimage that Nordica never
failed to make during a stay in London, and that
was to her mother's grave in Brompton Cemetery;
the mother to whose devotion her career owed so
much. That summer she took me with her. All the
flowers sent her at the opera the night before, and
more from a nearby florist were piled into the cab.
Filling her arms with them when our journey ended,
she led the way to a grave beside the farthest wall.

Getting down on her knees she cleared away dead
leaves and twigs from the flat tombstone; silent,
tearless, on her face that grand New England dignity of grief repressed. For a good hour she toiled,
then, rising, stood there for a long time silent, at last
saying softly, "I always like to think of her resting
here in the sunshine, for if there is any sunshine in
London 't finds this spot. I want some day to rest
here beside her."

At Claridge's Hotel one night, when Mr. Döme
kindly invited me to visit them at St. Moritz, she
whispered under her breath hurriedly, "Come,
come." Knowing that she needed me, I went. Mr.
Döme was young; he loved gaiety. At the Enga-

diner Hof in St. Moritz he and the rest of the party would remain downstairs to dance after dinner. Madame Nordica had to lie on a couch in her sitting-room. I would read to her.

The great singer's physical condition made the sight of strangers repellent; when people thrust themselves upon her as a celebrity, it became torture. All she asked was to be left alone with the few friends whom she knew thoroughly. Miss Cornélie Roosevelt-Scoville, now Countess Fabbricotti of Florence, was that year of our party, as she had been briefly the previous one at Menschenschwand. Of her Madame Nordica was extremely fond; the mere sight of her sunny youthfulness brought happiness.

Clyde Fitch, the dramatist, was at that time lying ill at an hotel below the cliff from us. Greatly admiring the man's witty mind, Madame Nordica, as soon as she grew stronger, would walk down to inquire after him, and very tired from the exertion would rest on my arm heavily as we toiled back. When he grew well enough to venture out, his first act was to bring her roses. The line he left with them was characteristic: "Some edelweiss that I have picked for you myself." It was a sly dig at those who bought edelweiss and then palmed it off as plucked personally on dizzy heights.

Presently, every sunny afternoon the Countess

Lonay, once Crown Princess Stéphanie of Austro-Hungary, would come up to the tennis court to watch Miss Roosevelt-Scoville play. With her came the Count, a colorless, inconsequent appearing person. The Countess, herself, bore traces of great former beauty only in her profile, for tragic experiences, which had hardened her expression savagely, could not alter that. Always, though, she appeared distinguished, especially in evening dress, for her figure had splendid lines and her carriage was noble.

Madame Patti we met unexpectedly one day out driving. Madame Nordica's carriage was coming from an opposite direction; the two meeting in a cloud of dust exchanged delighted greetings, ending in a choking fit and violent coughing that, during the opera season, would have cost them an appearance each. Beside Madame Patti sat Cederström; riding backwards on the front seat was Carolina. Carolina who for years had ruled as dictator, deciding even the dress that the diva should wear, whether or not she preferred it. The new husband had begun a new régime.

As the summer grew, and with it Madame Nordica's strength, we would wander among the shops in the lower village of St. Moritz. In one of them she stopped before a table piled with baby caps, handling each with wistful tenderness; in her face was hungry longing. We went home by the tram. Next her sat a tired, poor mother, a little one of three years on her lap. Leaning over, Madame Nordica took the baby, cuddling it comfortably against her breast, and very reluctantly she gave it back at the journey's end.

Frequent stays abroad had no relaxing effect upon either Madame Nordica's love or patriotism for her native land; always she remained a staunch American. The year of Queen Victoria's Diamond Jubilee, when I told her that I was going to London to lecture on American song composers, she exclaimed impetuously, "I am going to sing the program of songs as illustration for you!" And she did, out of patriotic interest.

The afternoon of it marked her first appearance after long absence from London; the audience was consequently brilliant. Her songs were by MacDowell, Chadwick, Beach, Foote, and the older of our composers. Prior to that, American songs were little known in London; to-day their omission from any vocal recital program there is a rarity. The initiative of Madame Nordica that afternoon went far toward establishing enduring interest in their beauty.

Madame Nordica sat on the stage behind a screen during the lecture that, as she told me, she might not miss a word. The mission was dear to my young heart; it had taken struggle to achieve it. And having achieved it, doubt assailed me as to whether or not I had gained my aim. Behind the screen Madame Nordica was waiting for me. What she said at that moment when I most needed encouragement shall never be forgotten. Do you wonder that I loved her, and now that she is gone no other singer can ever take her place?

The humorous side of things appealed delightfully to Madame Nordica. One afternoon during a Cincinnati Festival, she was to sing a Wagner excerpt. A whiteheaded old gentleman of the Committee came to her, and asked hesitantly, "Will you please sing a little louder than you did yesterday?"

"I couldn't," was her answer. "I gave out every bit of voice I had. Mr. Thomas drowned me out with the orchestra."

"Then I'll speak to him," said the old gentleman cheerfully, and trotted off. Very quickly he returned, red in the face.

"Well?" said Madame Nordica.

"He told me to go to the devil," the old gentleman blurted out.

"And so you came to me," was her smiling answer.

Alack and alas! It was a habit of Mr. Thomas' to drown out the singers, whom, apparently, he looked upon as his born enemies. Operatic excerpts he regarded as acquiring in concert more importance in the accompaniment than in the solo voice part, particularly in the case of Wagner.

Even Madame Materna, whose lung power equalled the might of a blacksmith's bellows, could not survive his orchestral thunderings in a Wagner program. In one such, when all was over, she turned to him scarlet with indignation, exclaiming loudly in German, "But, Mr. Thomas, that was a shame! That was a shame!"

Madame Nordica was always associated in companion parts with Jean de Reszke. Therefore an exciting night in her operatic life came with his reappearance at the Metropolitan, and after an attack of influenza which had kept him in retirement for a year. Indeed, at one time it was doubtful whether he would ever sing again. Arriving in New York, that doubt appeared still to assail the tenor.

A few days prior to his reappearance, Mr. de Reszke seemed anxious to tell me his ideas on voice training, which he declared he might some day follow, and in order that I might write about them. This made the situation look dubious; his mood was melting. However, when he did appear successfully, and I spoke of his earlier ardent wish, he scouted the idea, grandly announcing, "I shall follow my custom and give out nothing for publication."

That night of his return in *Lohengrin* at the Met-

ropolitan, this spirit of grand assurance was grandly
lacking. Even the call boy came near to an attack
of nerves at the sight of Jean's condition, while
Edouard de Reszke as *King Heinrich* could scarcely
hold his sword for trembling. Madame Nordica,
ignoring memory of her celebrated quarrel with
Jean over the confiscating of her rôle of *Brünnhilde*
in *Siegfried* and in favor of Madame Melba, suffered amicably along with the rest.

Coming on the stage in an atmosphere charged
with trepidation, Jean de Reszke's first tones were
veiled and insecure. The audience, bending forward in breathless stillness did not know whether
their beloved tenor had really returned with his
voice or without it. In the duet with *Elsa*, for-
getting self in its impassioned measures, the old
voice flashed out. With it mingled the golden tones
of Madame Nordica as *Elsa*.

At the act's end the scene was sensational. Not
content with simply bringing the pair out, both had
to parade the full breadth of the stage before the
curtain. Grandly he led her, and grandly she
walked beside him. Speaking of that moment later
Madame Nordica said laughingly, "If there is one
thing that I have, it is a tread." This was absolutely
true. It was regal, it was gracious. Born with the
New England angularity, which has made other
prima donnas from that section chronically clumsy,

Madame Nordica had freed herself from it by training. "If one has to reach a certain point," she once said to me, "it becomes not a question of getting there, but of *how* one gets there."

Madame Nordica had inherited a Pilgrim courage. This she proved many times. Once, on her way to the Auditorium Theatre to sing *Elsa*, a telegram was handed her announcing the death of her favorite niece, the only daughter of Mrs. George Walker, and gifted with a notable voice. Never did I see a more finished, touching impersonation of the part of *Elsa* than Nordica gave that day. Not a tear fell until after the opera was ended. Then she went to bed ill for three days.

On one occasion a torch held by a chorister in *Götterdämmerung* set fire to the long, flowing sleeve she wore. Continuing to sing the *Immolation* without pause she put out the flame with her bare hands. Again in *Götterdämmerung* and in that same *Immolation* with its constant change of key, there came to her an episode as irritating as it was hilarious. Holding *Brünnhilde's* steed *Grane* by his bridle, all was going well. Kept hungry, as all horses are before going on the stage, to make them docile, this *Grane* got a whiff of the cold cream spread thickly on the singer's arms. Slowly his rough tongue licked the length of one of them. She pushed him off, but he returned. He liked the diet. And his

LILLIAN NORDICA AS ELSA IN "LOHENGRIN"

late supper ended only with the scene, in which not a note of *Brünnhilde's* music had been missed.

Great as were Madame Nordica's triumphs in opera, her concert tours surpassed them in romance, for they brought her nearer to the people at large and close to their hearts.

She has told me of recitals in which her audience numbered more than the small town's population, people flocking from a distance to joy in her voice; she has told me of putting on a thousand dollar Paris gown by the light of a single kerosene lamp, and to go out before a crowded hall that cheered her every song.

There is a very precious memory that I treasure of a rehearsal of Verdi's *Requiem* at Madame Nordica's New York home, then in Madison Avenue. The other singers were Miss Edyth Walker, an American now dead, Andreas Dippel, and one of the great ones of that great epoch, Pol Plançon, now gathered into the beyond.

In the next room alone in the dark, I listened to such music and at such an hour. Ardently, Madame Nordica's lovely voice delivered its part in the *Agnus Dei;* then came the tender trio of the *Lux Aeterna.* At the words, "Let perpetual light shine upon them, O Lord, and grant them eternal rest," a myriad lights on the tower of Madison Square

Garden sprang into radiance against the blackness of the night.

Another memory, a very tender one, is connected with Madame Nordica's home at Ardsley-on-the-Hudson. It was at sunset, when all the summer world was flushed a dusky red. She was singing the *Suicide Aria* from *Gioconda*. Simmons at the piano was the only other person present. As the music grew in its intensity, a passionate, poignant despair welled in her singing; the outcry of a tortured heart, the premonition of bitter tragedy. Never have I heard her singing so impassioned. It became the death-cry of a soul. At its end, we three were still for a long time. Then she came to where I sat, and putting her hand on my head, said softly, "It has made me cry too." Turning, she went to a French window, standing there motionless, looking out into the growing dark; raising her arms with a gesture of passionate despair, she left the room without ˉpeaking.

Madame Nordica spoke one day in New York of her own end, and at a time of harrowing anxiety which made her, perhaps, think with longing of release. "At my funeral," she said, "I want a baritone to sing *Wotan's Farewell*, and an orchestra to play the *Funeral March* from *Götterdämmerung*. For me that music has such dear memories. And then I want some great speaker to say—to say—"

she broke off, for a moment pondering seriously, then changing her mood abruptly to one half-quizzical, added bluntly, "She did her damndest."

Sad reality brought no shadow of fulfillment of the great singer's wishes. Madame Nordica, shipwrecked in the Gulf of Papua on her projected singing journey around the world, arrived in Australia ill. Growing steadily worse, she struggled to reach the next point where she should sing, travelling wearily and by slow stages until she gained Batavia in the Dutch East Indies. There, in its cruel isolation, she perished.

Faithful Romayne Simmons, her accompanist, brought Madame Nordica's remains by tortuous route to London. After a church service and cremation there, her ashes were brought to this country by Mr. George W. Young, her husband. No funeral honors have been paid them here. Where the urn with those ashes rests has not been disclosed.

The American nation that she so honored by her singing in many lands has erected no memorial to the woman who loved so well her art, her country, and her people, and who served all three so loyally. Madame Nordica was the first of our prima donnas to sing the tremendous rôles of *Isolde*, the *Brünnhildes*, and *Kundry;* I know of no American woman singing them to-day. She sang in the foremost opera houses of Europe and of this country;

here, too, she sang in concert everywhere. Her singing life was a glorious romance. From poverty she rose through rare gifts and ardent toil to be crowned with a diamond tiara at the Metropolitan Opera House as Queen of Song. And she was beloved. Honored in life by her own countrymen and by kings and foreign peoples, today her very ashes appear to be denied a last Hail and Farewell.

CHAPTER IV

NELLIE MELBA

MADAME Melba's romance as the most acclaimed singer of the British Empire was long and glorious. In return she has given a splendid loyalty; her American tour during the World War, when she devoted every penny she received to her country's cause, was one proof of this. I have seen her in creations from the Rue de la Paix, her corsage encrusted with diamonds, but she appeared to me handsomer in those days of self-sacrifice, wearing her old gowns on the stage that she might have the price of new ones to add to her soldiers' fund.

The war itself meant to Madame Melba a very near and harrowing thing. Early in it she wrote to me from Australia, saying: "I have lost so many dear ones and so many friends in this cruel war— the world can never be the same again to me." Of her circle this was sadly true, for in England, as in all countries, the flower of the aristocracy had been the first to enlist and to fall.

During recent years much of the singer's time has been spent in Australia, where she has practically and nobly encouraged music. In her zenith Madame Melba's London home was a palace in Great Cumberland Place near the Marble Arch. Her admirers ranged from King Edward and Queen Alexandra to the crowds in waiting outside the gallery entrance at Covent Garden on nights when she sang there.

With vast means, for her earnings were doubled through skillful investments by the Rothschilds, she set out to plan a home. During her days of study in Paris with Madame Marchesi, the great Palace of Versailles had struck Melba's fancy. Buying the Great Cumberland Place house, she had its interior remodelled along Versailles lines. A small army of workmen, brought over from France, required two years to complete its wall decorations done in Cupids, garlands, and panels to hold paintings.

Furniture in keeping she selected personally, piece by piece; gilded chairs and sofas of the Louis periods; Aubosson carpets, pale blue and white, garlanded with faint pink roses; crystal chandeliers hung with pear-shaped pendants. The task in its elaborateness took her spare time for long.

Quarry Wood Cottage on the Thames near Maidenhead made then her summer home. It was a simple, charming place, overrun with cascades of *gloire de Dijon* roses. In the London social season, lasting from May until late July, she sang at Covent

To Mr Armstrong
from his sincere friend
Nellie Melba
1898

NELLIE MELBA

Garden, travelling up to town and back again after the performance.

Chauncey Depew came one day to Quarry Wood. Delighted with its roses, its clustering shade trees, its close-clipped lawn running to the river, he expressed a wish to stay.

"Then do," said Madame Melba.

"But I brought nothing with me," he retorted.

"Never mind that, we'll go shopping," suggested the diva. And they did, over at Maidenhead, the Senator returning with a night-shirt and tooth-brush as baggage.

There was always something very straightforward, very frank, very big-hearted about Madame Melba. Her Australian birth and rearing had left its unconventional impress. What she had to say she said directly and to the point. Her astounding frankness at out first meeting was, indeed, almost startling. "What family of Armstrongs do you belong to?" she asked bluntly. "My husband was an Armstrong and I abominated him."

Her motto was "Live and let live." She sustained it. Madame Melba had a broad way of overlooking irritating happenings even when they affected her stage success. Vignas, a Spanish tenor of the Grau régime, sang *Tannhäuser* to her *Elisabeth* the first and only time, I think, that she essayed the part. At that juncture the great success of Madame Nordica and Jean de Reszke in Wagner had set the other prima donnas aflame to sing his music. Even Madame Calvé announced that she would sing *Isolde*, later, though she could never get the time right in certain ensembles of Berlioz's *Faust*.

In the circumstances Madame Melba had fixed high hopes on her *Elisabeth*. Vignas with the influenza risked singing *Tannhäuser* and wrecked the performance. Only as far as *Wolfram's* "Evening Star" did it get, and then the curtain had to be rung down. Mr. Grau made a little speech, saying that Madame Melba to extend the program would sing *Lucia's* Mad Scene. Which she did, in the costume of *Elisabeth*, crown and all. Every other artist in the cast looked on Vignas' foolhardy risk and consequent defection as a personal affront. Madame Melba, the most seriously affected of any, alone came vigorously to his defence.

Madame Melba did not always attain to the angelic. Then she was amusing. Massenet's *Werther* had its American première at Chicago. Madame Eames was the *Charlotte*. Neither Melba nor Calvé just then loved her. Wonderfully gowned the pair sat in a lower box. Before them on its upholstered rail rested a score of *Werther*, upside down. But that the public did not know. Neither did Eames.

Every little while, first Calve then Melba would shoot out a disapproving forefinger at some spot on

the score and raise her eyebrows. Being much observed, a vastly interested public began to watch for
mistakes too. That Madame Eames knew what
was going on, no doubt remained. Her increasing
stiffness and angularity proclaimed it. But not being on speaking terms with the two ladies, she could
not tell them later what she thought.

No prima donna escapes her evil quarters of an
hour. A most trying episode came to Madame
Melba, herself, in that same Chicago where she was
accustomed to wild enthusiasm. The Committee of
a sectarian hospital had engaged her to give a benefit
concert for their institution. The program was of
operatic selections. Many tickets had been sold to
people of the congregation, who had, perhaps, never
heard an opera. And thriftily they used their tickets
to get their money's worth.

The solemn frigidity of that audience could
scarcely have been greater; rigid and unbending it
sat in silence. Not until the Mad Scene came was
it prodded into enthusiasm. Seizing the moment,
I went behind the scenes to ask after Madame
Melba's health.

Coincident with my arrival there was rolled into
her dressing-room a big, upright clothes basket, of
the kind that holds bushels. From its top spouted a
quantity of American Beauty Roses. "What is that
damned thing?" called Madame Melba, just as the

leading nose of the Hospital Committee, which had contributed this floral offering, appeared in the doorway.

To prima donna subtleties Madame Melba was a stranger. When she said a thing, nothing was left to her hearer's imagination. Shortly after Madame Nordica's death, I went to London to say good-bye to Melba, who was sailing for Australia. Her first words were regarding the great American's sad end.

Shipwreck in the Gulf of Papua on her way to Australia had put Nordica in no condition to sing, especially before strange audiences. Her reception on arriving in that country had been icy. This Melba resented, feeling that Nordica's great art alone deserved their hearty recognition. "They murdered her in Australia," cried Melba passionately, her eyes full of tears, "and I shall tell them so when I get back!" Doubtless she did.

At one time there had been estrangement between the prima donnas. But that was completely blotted from Melba's mind; her one thought was of her dead colleague's greatness. Madame Melba was splendidly fearless. She hesitated as little to tell a nation as she did an individual what she felt to be the truth.

None could travel about the globe as did this diva without meeting exciting adventures on the way. By chance, I experienced one of these with her. It came at the California Theatre at San Francisco, and during her first concert tour of the Pacific coast. There were ill omens that night as prelude to the final climax. During an act from *Rigoletto*, pipes burst under the stage, sending up a cloud of steam that made the place look like a scene from *Walküre*. The curtain was rung down immediately and repairs started.

Finally, when all was supposed rectified, up the curtain went again on the exact spot that *Rigoletto* had left off. The program was long, and so they were economical. Being like all plumbers, the men had left something undone. So great hammering under the stage mingled with the singing on it. Madame Melba came off furious and nervous, vowing she would go home. The house was packed. After great persuasion she decided to remain; going to her dressing-room, she changed *Gilda*'s costume for that of *Lucia*, whose Mad Scene was to follow.

Presently, when Melba took her place behind the scenes, increasing nervousness set in. Twice she exclaimed, "I am going to faint!" Leaving me alone with her, Miss Bennet, her companion, went for a glass of water. While she was gone a great outcry started in the audience. People began climbing over the footlights, pushing aside the curtain, which was down, and running across the stage on that side next an exit. By flashes, the swinging curtain disclosed a glare of fire in the auditorium. Madame Melba, in her *Lucia* costume, her hair about her shoulders, and nearly fainting, gave in that moment a pretty fine example of British pluck. Not knowing the real cause of trouble, she started staggering through the wings; she knew that something had happened in the audience, and her one idea was to go out and quiet it.

By that time Miss Bennet had returned. Each with an arm about the diva we were leading her back, when Charles Ellis, her manager, and Rigo, the stage director, grabbed her from us and made toward the stage entrance.

Someone rolled up the curtain. With that a mob came struggling across the footlights onto the stage: Orchestra players, their instruments hugged in their arms; ladies in torn evening gowns; men, helping and helped.

From the orchestra pit rose a frantic cry, "My hat and my harp! My hat and my harp!" It came from a woman harpist in whose mind these treasures remained uppermost. The aide-de-camp of Prince Albert, now King of Belgium, and who had remained behind the scenes during the concert, gallantly rushed to her rescue, dragging lady, harp, and hat over the footlights. Next morning an enterprising newspaper carried in its columns a sketch of the

incident. It showed two heroic workmen saving a
lady in distress.

Subjects for more authentic sketches were not
lacking. The tenor, Salignac, later of the Paris
Opéra Comique, and dressed as *Faust* for the Garden
Scene, was sent home in a cab; Leo Rains, subse-
quently long at the Berlin Royal Opera, started off
afoot to his hotel wearing over his *Mephisto* costume
a mackintosh reaching only to his knees.

Another proof that I recall of Madame Melba's
courage came at the Chicago Auditorium on the
night when a madman sprang upon the stage. The
curtain had just risen on the Balcony Scene in
Romeo and Juliet. Melba was the *Juliet;* Jean de
Reszke was singing *Romeo*. Running swiftly down
a side aisle, and reaching the stage by way of a little
stairway leading from the great organ, the lunatic
was behind the footlights almost before any saw
him. In a few minutes, though it seemed much
longer, the poor wretch had been dragged off.

Meanwhile, neither Melba nor de Reszke budged
from their pose, although, quite near them, four
husky stage-hands were struggling to overpower and
drag away the lunatic. When the orchestra began
again, Madame Melba's tones, at first a trifle tremu-
lous, gave no further sign of nervous strain; Jean
de Reszke's voice had not a fraction of unsteadiness.

How many singers are there whose training would bring such perfect breath control?

Loyal to those she really loved, just as she was loyal to her country, Madame Melba's allegiance to her great teacher, Madame Marchesi, never swerved. And Marchesi prized it. "Of the many I have taught," she once said to me, "those who have been grateful I could count on the fingers of one hand." She alluded, I know, to the greater ones.

Presently, she told me of Eames who had studied with her, and later, over her own signature, written against her; she told of Calvé who had made her début and later her successes as a Marchesi pupil, and then gone to another teacher.

Calvé's unsought excuse for this came in a note to Marchesi, saying that her countrymen would feel more kindly toward her if she sang to them as a pupil of one born in France. This honor not falling to Madame Marchesi, who hailed from Frankfort, precluded her in Calvé's narrow vision from a credit in which musical history will be more generous.

Madame Melba, when she came to Paris in her golden days, often made her home at Madame Marchesi's in the Rue Jouffroy. If she did not stop there, her first pilgrimage on arriving in the city was to her teacher. The diva's radiant career made a vital link with the life Marchesi loved and which she, as one of the great women of the nineteenth

SALVATORE MARCHESI AND MATHILDE MARCHESI

century, had lived actively so long. And to the end, Melba made her feel how important a part she had played in her success.

In Marchesi's zenith, managers flocked to the musical evenings at her studio and in search of rising "stars." Emma Nevada and Sybil Sanderson had been pupils there; the trio, Melba, Calvé, Eames made their successful débuts later. Long prior to that, and before leaving Vienna for the French capital, Marchesi had taught Ilma de Murska and Etelka Gerster. Only a tithe of the singing celebrities that Marchesi trained, however, were known to us in America, for they came to her from Russia, South America, England and Australia, as well as from the United States.

Gounod, Rubinstein, Massenet, the great statesmen of France, and people of the Paris world of society and letters helped make Marchesi's *soirées* there memorable. In them young girls, presently renowned, sang as pupils. When the dusk fell in her long and brilliant life, people melted away from the house in the Rue Jouffroy. "Even my colleagues never darken my doorway," she once said to me passionately. "I am not French, so I am not of them."

Through it all, Melba remained touchingly, splendidly loyal. Always she was sending pupils to Marchesi, always she was trying to find engagements for any who proved promising. Her great influence, especially at the Covent Garden Opera, made itself practically felt. It is at once a great joy and simple justice to chronicle this sympathetic, enduring association between Melba and Marchesi. That association, in itself, is sufficient reason for including memories of the one with memories of the other. In musical biography, written so often without an intimate, personal knowledge, the finer things in a great musician's life are not recorded, leaving as a result merely a formal story of brilliant successes.

Madame Melba, it was, who sent me with a letter of introduction to Madame Marchesi, for which I am strongly grateful. In turn, Marchesi gave me a letter to Leschetizky, who received me charmingly at his home in Vienna. "What kind of a man is Leschetizky?" Marchesi asked me when I called to thank her on returning. My look of surprise at this, coming from the person who had introduced me, must have been transparent, for she added with that slow, droll smile of hers, "I have never met him. But that is unnecessary. We artists understand one another."

Madame Marchesi's married life with the Marquis de la Rajata de Castrone was a happy one, and their devotion beautiful. Calling in the Rue Jouffroy one morning, she asked me, "When did you ᵎ arrive in Paris?"

"Yesterday," was the answer.

"And you came to see me to-day?"

"Yes, because I love you."

"But you have never made me a declaration," she retorted, her eyes twinkling.

"I'll do it now," I answered, promptly getting down on my knees.

"Salvatore! Salvatore!" she called to her husband, "come here. I am having a proposal."

In he came, smiling. "Ah, my dear," he said to her, "it is your intellect that he is in love with." And he looked at her with the fond eyes of twenty-one. At that time they had been married fifty-three years.

One night Madame Marchesi invited me to go with them to the Opéra Comique. Madame Alda, a young thing, slender and beautiful, just in from a Brussels engagement, was the only other present in their loge. After the curtain fell, as Madame Marchesi was going down the long stairway, leaning on my arm, she said something unforgettable, something that made me feel humbly proud: "I am sorry, my friend, that we did not meet earlier. But we sincere people manage to find each other in this world, don't we?"

Some time after her husband's death, I was dining with Madame Marchesi. She had been talking in the gay, bantering way that she so bravely kept up still.

Abruptly, she began to speak about the past, and those near to her who were gone, among them her uncle Baron Haussmann. He, under Napoleon III, had founded the beauty of Paris as we know it to-day. To Marchesi he had been for years a rock of reliance. Of one and then another she spoke, suddenly throwing up her hands with tragic gesture to exclaim, "They are all gone, all gone, leaving me alone," and she wept bitterly.

That was the period, too, when her friends as well had faded from her, one by one, but never the faithful Melba. Knowing of all this, and much more besides, I tried to say as lightly as the poignant moment would allow, "Never mind, Madame Marchesi, I'll come to the Rue Jouffroy and stop with you."

Taking me literally, she answered, "I would love to have you. But it wouldn't do. It wouldn't do. People might talk." She must then have been long past eighty. Perhaps, though, she was worldly-wiser than I. She had lived long in Paris.

Madame Marchesi had outlived all her children save one, Blanche, married to Baron Caccamisi and living in London. Resembling her father, and very handsome, her voice had received the devoted training of her mother.

Another tragedy that life brought presently to Marchesi was the outliving of that activity of mind which had added to her glorious fame. But curiously enough, even when the time came that her mental vision was not clear, she could teach as well as ever. That one passion of her life was mercifully spared the longest. The last of her pupils' auditions that I heard in the Salle Hoche proved this. Many beautiful voices, beautifully trained, sang that day. But they sang too long. Failing to time the numbers beforehand, her program, which began at half-past two o'clock, lasted until after six.

Presently a cloud obscured Marchesi's once brilliant intellect. But even then she taught me of her wisdom. One afternoon, though weak, a desire came to her to show and explain to me her autograph album. The book was filled with tributes from statesmen, painters, composers, singers. Some names she would pass by impatiently, saying, "They did not live." At others she would pause, and say gently, "They are immortal."

Living to a preternaturally old age, Madame Marchesi's memories extended from the time of Mendelssohn; she had seen many rise to greatness; the fame of few had survived them. And so, in turning over the leaves of her album that afternoon, she passed many, once famous, impatiently, and stopped at few to say, "They are immortal."

Her observation of the horde of pupils that passed through her studio deepened Marchesi's insight. Talking of the psychology of singers, and how fully she understood them, she said, "While a girl is studying her *vocalises* she is the soul of tractable docility, but the moment she gets an aria, and before she knows how to sing it, she begins to put on prima donna airs."

Another comment of hers was, "I have never yet had a pupil of good family who became an actress. Always having been trained conventionally, always restrained, freedom of emotional expression died. On the other hand, girls not well born, not brought up in a restricted conventionality, gave full play to emotional expression on the stage. And they were actresses."

A woman who had lived in Paris at the same *pension* with Melba in her student days at Marchesi's studio, told me of the future diva's earliest triumph. She had been asked to sing at a great house and in a musicale to which the grand world of Paris had been invited. "I was reading very late," the story ran, "and a light still shone above my door. A timid knock came. And there stood Nellie Melba in a simple white frock and tears. 'I had to tell someone,' she explained. And then related how people had that night gone mad over her singing, and an old French general had rushed up to embrace and kiss her, crying, 'You are already one of the great ones of the world!'"

While she was studying *Mimi* in Puccini's *La Bohême*, I happened in her New York sitting-room one day. Melba was all enthusiasm. Going to the piano she went through *Mimi's* music from the score, playing her own accompaniment, for in her girlhood she had studied the piano. Special portions of the rôle which appealed most strongly, she would repeat, and afterward exclaim upon their beauty. In later years, she very often sang the part, one without a single flourish of vocal display, and in preference to any other.

But how she shone in florid Italian music! The absolute assurance; the audacity; the perfection of her trill; the pearl-like evenness of her scales, not only in tone quality, but in tone duration; her exquisite *pianissimo* on open tones in alt; her dazzling delivery of bravura passages flung out with a spontaneous certainty that was fabulous. Preëminent in her field, Madame Melba reigned, as did Madame Patti, in a kingdom all her own.

CHAPTER V

ERNESTINE SCHUMANN-HEINK

FOR forty years Madame Schumann-Heink has sung in public. Her great colleagues retired or vanished, she still splendidly maintains her place in art and in people's hearts.

Her courage and endurance are phenomenal; where others cease, she only fairly starts, for her superb physique is supplemented with a will that knows no breaking.

It was life as she lived it that developed her. Born to an Austrian father and an Italian mother, she inherited a gaiety of spirit that was indestructible, come what might. Bubbling over with a youthfulness that she still sustains so freshly, her hardships have been met with a heart that was unafraid.

At the outset there was nothing to promise that her talents would find help to recognition, but she took each little chance as it came. The first one arrived with the discovery of her voice, which was made at the Ursuline Convent in Prague, an institution combining philanthropy with its curriculum. The Choir there, all of girls' and women's voices,

To my dearest friend
"William Armstrong" with
Gratitude, affection and love.

Ernestine Schumann-Heink.

New York,
May 1918.

© MOFFETT CHICAGO
1912.

ERNESTINE SCHUMANN-HEINK

was directed by the good Sister Martha Bernadine, with Sister Martha Angelina as organist; recognizing the 'cello tones in the new pupil's throat, they put her to singing in church services.

Other worshippers came besides the nuns and their pupils on Sundays and holidays, when Ernestine, the Madame Schumann-Heink of to-day, sang with the rest in the choir-loft. By great fortune to her, for it meant the opening of her whole career, there came one afternoon to Vespers a retired prima donna, once a singer at the Paris Opéra. Her quick, musical ear caught the rich voice of the girl, and when the service was ended she put the nuns and their charges into a flutter by trailing her laces and grand air up the choir stairs and into their midst. Unfortunately, Madame Schumann-Heink cannot remember the name of the woman who that day turned her life into a new channel by mounting the stairs to tell her that her voice was beautiful, and with the big heart of the artist offering to give her free lessons.

One visit and the dream was ended; Ernestine's father was ordered to Gratz. This time it was etiquette instead of the exercise of piety that brought its reward. Calling, as was customary, on the wives of her husband's superior officers at the new station, Madame Schumann-Heink's mother came to the house of the Colonel. His wife, a motherly soul, listened to the story of the voice, the interrupted lessons, and the hopes that were shattered. She, too, had daughters, and knew the limitations of purses military; one of her own offspring had been trained for the operatic stage, but, failing in that career, had taken to teaching.

There are plenty of good hearts in the world, and Mademoiselle Le Claire, for that was the stage name of the daughter whose voice had failed to keep her there, had one of them. The new officer's wife dried her tears, and took home another offer of free lessons.

Ernestine, who seems never to have looked on the removal as tragic and the end of all things, climbed the stairs to the Colonel's daughter for three years for lessons. During one of them, a tenor, later successful, heard her sing in the room adjoining that in which he was waiting. Being of critical vein he asked Mademoiselle Le Claire, "Who is the young singer with a voice like a calf?"

"She will one day be among the world's greatest contraltos," was the answer he got. Later, while the girl was proving this prediction, he did her a good turn when he could.

Hard enough days had come between. Ernestine, being the eldest of many children, felt the brunt of them. The running of errands fell to her lot. Those to the grocer, though frequent, were not the pleasantest. To get credit of him at times when he grudged it, she would sing songs. Unfailingly they brought the desired commodities. Tiring of this wheedling process, and being, it seems, always practical, she set out unknown to her parents to earn something herself.

Across from her home was a restaurant where peasants danced away otherwise boring Sunday afternoons. A pianist was needed. Ernestine applied and was accepted. The fee was an equivalent of fifty cents. But fifty cents would buy some cash groceries.

Several of these professional engagements were fulfilled, and successfully, before news of them reached her horrified parents. "The child, the *daughter* of an army officer, play for peasants to dance at a restaurant!" The thought overwhelmed them.

"Why not? We need the money," was Ernestine's retort. But her piano playing ceased.

At sixteen Ernestine was ready for her début, singing at Gratz as one of the quartet in a performance of Beethoven's Ninth Symphony. Frau Marie Wilt, the soprano of the occasion, was delighted with the new contralto, and promised to introduce her in Vienna. This was more easily proposed than accepted; the officer's salary of thirty dollars a month did not allow many tours for his daughters.

But when Field Marshal von Benedick, who had fought with him in the campaign of " '66" in Italy, heard that the child of a comrade was about to lose a fine opportunity, he came to the rescue with a pocketbook less full than the gold braid on his uniform would outwardly warrant. So Ernestine, chaperoned by Mademoiselle Le Claire, set out for Vienna. There, accompanied by Frau Wilt, she sang for the Imperial-Royal-Court-Intendant Jauner.

The shoes that the young singer wore that day were a trophy from the barracks at Gratz. Like those of her younger sisters, they were made from the scraps of leather left over from soldiers' brogans, and cost nothing. Clomping across the parquette floor, in a dress that reached to her ankles, she entered her judge's dandified presence. Mutual aversion was instant. Ernestine could not sing any more than Jauner could listen, and she went back to Gratz with no visible result from spending the Field Marshal's money.

At sixteen one cannot remain unhappy very long. Shortly there was ground for light-heartedness. A month later she was able to make another journey, this time to Dresden, to enter in competition for a vacant post at the Royal Opera there. Fate was kinder than at Vienna. Two other applicants sang, but she was the one chosen for a three years' contract.

Her first appearance was as *Azucena* in Verdi's
Il Trovatore, and she laughed all through the performance. "Because," as she told me, "so many
people were there and my salary, sixty dollars a
month, was double that of my father's for drilling
his soldiers."

At that early day she sang her rôles by ear, they
came to her out of the air, as it were, for no great
amount of musical knowledge bothered her, as it
did a certain old oboe player in the orchestra who
toiled for every atom of it that he got. Viewing the
young contralto, laughing as *Azucena* in captivity
and all the rest of her dismal moments; getting a
new part without a tithe of the labor that he had in
learning a *cadenza*, he promptly announced that
she would never amount to anything as a singer.
Having a good share of that antipathy which the
orchestral player so frequently has for the easier
success of the vocalist, he told her so. At the time
her heart was too gay to take him seriously, but in
a critical moment of disaster later she remembered
it.

Part of her duties was to sing in the Cathedral.
One great feast day, Corpus Christi it was, the King
and Queen of Saxony and their court marched in
procession to a Mass for which great musical preparations had been made. All went well until Ernestine's first solo came. Lost in wonder at the scene,

and the sight of "so many beautiful young lieu-
tenants," as she described it, the new contralto forgot that such things as solos existed. A poke from
Court Director Krebs' baton brought her back to
reality. The old oboe player, blowing in conscien-
tious horror, sat quite near her. An unheeding
past, and his dismal prediction swept over Ernestine
to combine with the fright of the present.

Tones came not written in the music, she made
a fresh haphazard start, but even the time she struck
on was different from the one in which the orchestra
was playing. Down came the Court Conductor's
baton on her shoulders. "Crazy goose," were the
words that accompanied it.

After that followed a long season of sack-cloth
and ashes. For four years she was made to sing
under Franz Wüllner's direction at Vespers on week
days, when the congregation, made up chiefly of
old ladies, was supposed to constitute proof against
lapse of memory. A great teacher, she owes to
Wüllner her first real musical awakening.

Her new mentor understood better than did she
what was needed. Before that she had sung purely
by ear, not knowing two-four time from six-eight.
He made her sing in turn the soprano, alto, tenor
and bass in the Vespers, and always at sight. This,
with the training she got at the opera, gave a
new turn to her art, a turn that began with the de-

scent of Krebs' baton in the Cathedral at Dresden.

Meanwhile, the old oboe player, being of a frank and musical nature, repeated his dire predictions in season and out. When she returned from her first successful engagement in London to sing again in Dresden, she said to him, "Well, I *have* amounted to something, haven't I?"

"The newspapers say so," he answered with niggardly tartness, "but how do I *know* it?"

Between those Dresden days and the engagement, which, signed in London, brought her to America and great good fortune, came a bitter period. She was then singing at the Hamburg Stadt Theatre at a pitiably small salary. Her rôles ranged from Mozart to Verdi, from Wagner to Bizet, whose *Carmen* was one of her parts. Married at that time to Lieutenant Heink, a Prussian officer, he gambled away a good share of her earnings. With a baby on one arm, and holding an opera score that she was studying, she would stop to stir the dinnerpot boiling on the stove.

Through the gloom a ray of hope pierced finally. A benefit performance was to take place at Berlin. The bill was *Il Trovatore;* she was invited to sing *Azucena.* No fee, not even her expenses, was offered. But it meant a loophole of escape. So she travelled there by night, third class.

The hour of arrival being early, she sat on a bench

in the Tiergarten until time for rehearsal came
around, being too poor to afford a room at an hotel.
Later, when her plight became known at the opera
house, she was given the money to pay for her
lodging.   Before she slept that night, however,
her voice had aroused a sensation in Berlin.

To-day, Madame Schumann-Heink is one of the
richest of world prima donnas; but for her first meeting in London with Maurice Grau, then manager
of the Metropolitan, Madame Nordica loaned her
a long-trained silk gown to wear and much jewelry.
This was done to make the contralto appear a person
of moneyed-success, which would mean better terms
in the contract.

In America, her success was immediate and con-
vincing.   From the outset, Madame Schumann-
Heink lived in the utmost simplicity.   Other prima
donnas, in those golden days, sustained the style of
princesses.   The great contralto made her home at
a little hotel called Belvedere, now vanished, a
great building standing on its site at the corner of
Fourth Avenue and Eighteenth Street.

That little hotel had its traditions.   When the
Academy of Music was New York's operatic mecca,
the great ones of song made the Hotel Belvedere
their stopping place.   Faded photographs of them
hung on its walls as souvenirs.   There was, however, among the few contemporary ones, the portrait

of a prima donna whom many will recall, the radiantly beautiful Marie Engle. It was made in Dublin when she was singing in Mapleson's company as a colleague of Madame Nordica. Later she appeared often at Covent Garden; following that she came to New York's Metropolitan, singing between times at Covent Garden during the London season, and, finally, going to the Royal Opera, Madrid. Her voice, though ample, was not large, but lovely in quality and exquisitely trained. She was one of the most beautiful women of her day in opera.

Forsaking her career when her father fell ill, she went to him at an isolated farm-house in Michigan, nursing him faithfully through a bitter winter. To heighten the pathos of her loneliness, he, wandering at times in his mind, would tell her of his beautiful daughter Marie, so far away and whom he longed so hungrily to see. When death came to Mr. Engle, she forsook the world as she had forsaken opera. Becoming a devout Catholic, her days have since been given to tirelessly doing good. In all prima donna history there is, perhaps, no such romance as this one of dear Marie Engle.

Living then myself at the Hotel Belvedere, I quickly learned the invaluable aid given Madame Schumann-Heink by her husband, Mr. Schumann, now dead. He it was who laid the foundation of her fame as a *lieder* singer. Ferdinand, their son, told me that when the children were quite small and perforce left behind at the Villa Tini in Dresden, their father would sit at the piano at twilight, his little ones about him, and play on it the story of what their great singing mother was doing at that hour in New York: Now she leaving for the opera; now the orchestra was starting and *Elsa* would enter; now with the great duet in the second act they must listen closely to hear mother's splendid voice as *Ortrud.* Perhaps the children needed no such reminder to keep "mother" freshly alive in their hearts, but it was beautiful and it was poetic. To have heard Mr. Schumann give in words the interpretation of a *lied*, was to know that in him lay richly those two qualities.

There was a trait with Mr. Schumann, though, that was sometimes inconvenient; he was furiously jealous. One night at the Metropolitan, the Shepherd in *Tannhäuser vanished.* Where he went or what ailed him, disturbed no one; the absence of any substitute, however, did. When the curtain went up on the Wartburg there stood Madame Schumann-Heink behind a pile of rocks which left only her head visible. Such a roguish boy Shepherd she made, and such singing of his one song has, doubtless, not been heard before or since in New York.

"But why a Shepherd without arms or legs?" I asked her later.

"That's just it, without legs," and she almost strangled with laughter.

"Schumann's so jealous he would not let me show them. That's why he hid all but my head behind a pile of stage rocks."

After the children grew old enough to be brought here from Germany, Madame Schumann-Heink made a real home for them. I have known her to travel a thousand miles to spend a single day under her own rooftree. And always she brought each child a present. At such times at dinner, where the long table barely sufficed for her own brood and a friend or two, after saying grace she would raise her eyes reverently, exclaiming, "Thank God that my children and I are together." Then winking the tears back, she would proceed to fill many plates.

Madame Schumann-Heink's romance has been a double one; that of great singer and noble mother. But never did she seem to lose sight of the one in the other. There have been harrowing scenes, though, in that dual life of hers, in which her burden of sentiment, the prize gift of a singer, made them more harrowing still. One such I recall. It came when her home was at Ludlow, near New York, where I had gone on a stormy night to say good-bye before she left for a long tour. George Washington, a strapping fellow now, but a very little fellow then, knew what was coming. He said nothing, keeping up stoutly, but his white face looked pinched.

Some new records of hers had just arrived; Madame Schumann-Heink set them to going. Suddenly, her eyes fell on George. Creeping into a corner, he lay huddled there weeping his heart out. The sound of mother's voice, added to the thought of parting, had been too much for him. Taking him in her arms and cuddling him close, she rocked to and fro with streaming eyes. As I slipped out, she waved one hand in a desolate good-bye.

When the children were grown or growing up, Madame Schumann-Heink's home on the crest of Caldwell's Mountain, in New Jersey, was the one which she had bought with profits from a single season in light opera. Once, on a happy day I spent there, the great contralto just in from one tour and due to leave the next day on another, Mizzi, her only daughter, reached sudden, irrevocable decision. It arrived in the middle of dinner. Putting down her knife and fork, she announced solemnly, "Mother, I'm not going to leave you until I am old. I won't marry at all till I am twenty-eight."

But Mizzi forgot her promise much earlier. She has now two fine children of her own, who, when they visit grandmother at the Waldorf, find life a series of grand surprises, with fruit growing on every window-sill where she has hidden it exactly on a level with their searching eyes.

Following dinner in the Caldwell's Mountain days the singer's first advice to the older sons, whom she had given pipes, was, "Now, boys, fill up and smoke." That finished, rugs would be tossed aside, Mrs. Hoffman, her faithful accompanist, would play ragtime, and Madame Schumann-Heink would dance tirelessly until every boy there had had his turn. Ringing choruses came next, not classical gems but popular things, like *Everybody's Doing It* or *There'll be a Hot Time in the Old Town To-night*.

That is all ended now. One afternoon I stopped at the Waldorf to see Madame Schumann-Heink. Her mood was one of abject desolation. "I have just gotten back from Caldwell's Mountain," she said, a catch in her breath. "All are married now but George, and he's at school. I've sold the place for there's not one child left to live with me." The same old tragedy, played in the same old way, just as it has been from the world's beginning.

Madame Schumann-Heink's life is ever active; aside from her art it touches vitally at many vital points, for her interest remains indefatigable and human. But always there must exist with her the aching void which comes to every noble mother whose chief aim through long, hard years has been to make a home for those she loved, only at last to find herself alone in it.

It has been many years since the great contralto was heard in Wagner's music dramas in this country. At Munich's *Prinz Regenten Theatre*, I listened to her last as *Waltraute* in *Götterdämmerung*. At no time had she previously attained such heights as on that afternoon. Years of *lieder* and song singing had added to her work a charm in elaborate detail that was magical in its effect. Word, nuance, phrase, polished to the utmost without disturbing the broad, sustained outline of the whole, became as marvellous filigrees. Those beside her on the stage seemed raw by contrast with the revelation that she gave of what Wagner's music really held.

When *Waltraute's* music ceased that day, *Götterdämmerung* ended for me. Meeting Madame Schumann-Heink at the stage entrance, she invited me to drive back with her. Mr. Rapp, whom she had not yet divorced, was along. The vehicle proved to be one of those victorias, which still flourish in Europe as instruments of torture.

Instead of sitting on the bird-perch which served as front seat, Madame Schumann-Heink insisted that I sit on Rapp's lap. I found he had none. His waistcoat buttons seemed to touch his knees. All who know Munich know the steep incline leading from the *Prinz Regenten Theatre* downward toward the river Iser. In making that descent, constantly admonished by the singer to "Sit back! Sit back!" it became a question of which stopping place I should reach first, Hotel Vier Jahreszeiten or the river.

During the World War, Madame Schumann-Heink sang at Camp Dix. That afternoon she took me with her. The way was long and we landed shortly before six o'clock, the hour set for the concert. One of the General's staff met her to say that dinner awaited us at headquarters. "Doesn't he know yet that I cannot eat before singing?" was her announcement. So the rest of us, famished from the long drive, went hungry until late that night.

It was a red sunset. The vast plain where the camp rested was as bare as that space which in North Prussia they call the Sandbox of the Holy Roman Empire. It was crowded with hideous buildings, hastily erected. No mining town could have looked worse. That was the last picture of home which many a fine boy carried away, and to die with it in his heart.

Looking out on the mass of soldiers, already crowded rank on rank to hear her, a spasm of pain crossed the face of Madame Schumann-Heink. "Oh! that such boys should be feed for cannon!" she said despairingly. And then, with her brightest smile, went out to sing to them.

To me it was the most solemn hour that I have lived through. There were no lofty cathedral arches lost in misty shadows; no air heavy with long said, passionate prayers and burning incense. Only a vast, sandy plain, and a red sunset slowly fading into ghostly dusk. It meant war; it meant heroic, inescapable resolve; it meant bloody battlefields to come, and the bringing to many of an eternal dusk. If an impressionist scene-painter had planned bald setting for this prelude to tragedy at once heroic, terrible, he could not have chosen better.

Against this setting Madame Schumann-Heink sang with her soul in songs of home, of mother, and of cheer; Bach's "Heart Ever Faithful" lending a touch of sublime trust in the Great Protector. But it was the words of "mother" songs which sank the deepest. Many a boy, as he listened there, brushed away tears sneakingly with a grimy hand.

This was Madame Schumann-Heink's self-chosen mission throughout the war. Unsparing of her strength, regardless of voice-wrecking singing in the open air, she went from camp to camp untiringly, the motherliness in her own big heart bringing very near to each listening boy that mother whom he had left behind.

In all great American centers Madame Schumann-Heink has sung in opera. Everywhere throughout this country she has sung in concert not once, but many times. She has sung both the classics and the simple songs of the people in townlets and at Chautauquas, where mothers listened as they nursed their babies; she has sung in vast halls where trained music lovers joyed in her *lieder*. Everywhere she has had triumphs; everywhere she is beloved. Twelve American municipalities have bestowed on her the Freedom of the City. The scenes that she has aroused have likely been unparalleled in musical history.

In one recital at Denver, Colorado, her audience numbered fourteen thousand, while twenty-five thousand strove vainly to enter; at Camp Kearney, California, one hundred thousand soldiers thronged to hear her; at Cleveland, Ohio, in a Sunrise Service on Memorial Day, she sang to even more. All this is but a small part of Ernestine Schumann-Heink's noble singing romance.

And she remains supremely human. These lines came in answer to a letter, the first she had had from me in months:

BELOVED DEAR FRIEND:
It's too peculiar; since weeks I have been thinking of you, and I was really worried—and you have your dear mother with you; God love you both——

The letter stopped short there. She had fallen suddenly ill with pneumonia. Still remembering the letter, she had asked Mr. Frank La Forge, on that tour her accompanist, to forward it to me as it was.

CHAPTER VI

IGNACE JAN PADEREWSKI

NO musican in history has been granted a romance such as that of Ignace Jan Paderewski: The world's most beloved pianist; the Premier of Poland; Delegate from his country to the League of Nations.

It was in his heyday as pianist that I first learned to know the great Pole, and it was away from the world, away almost from music itself that there were lived out at Villa Riond-Bosson my most delightful memories of him.

Since those days his feet have trodden rugged ways as world figure in politics, but Paderewski is philosopher as well as optimist; that combination may have gone far toward leaving his beautiful heart unsoured by hard experience.

Riond-Bosson, where he knew the best peace and happiness that life has given him, owns a romance all its own. It was in the time of the French Revolution that Marquis des Tournelles fled to Morges on the Swiss side of Lake Geneva, when his sovereign, Louis XVI, and Queen Marie Antoinette lost their heads under the guillotine. Saving not only his own head, but a portion of his fortune, he was able to live out his natural life at the Villa Riond-Bosson which he built him.

The choice of its location was ideal, a crest of land running down into the lake's blue waters, with a view of the Savoy Mountains of his homeland rising on the far side, and farther away still Mont Blanc's glistening peaks. Morges starts almost at the villa's tall-pillared gates, and ends at a quay undisturbed except when stray passengers alight from the boat plying between Geneva and Lausanne. And Morges itself is one of those spotless little Swiss towns that are filled with blooming rose trees the summer long.

All this makes romance enough, but there is more of it in the villa's history, prior to Paderewski's purchase of the property. The old Marquis' son, who went away to fight under Napoleon the Great, came back a general. From then on he resided at the villa, as did his children and grandchildren after him. Finally the property fell into the hands of Count Le Marois.

He, by some unfortunate chance, postponed marriage until his scalp came through the hair of his head; at that juncture he found him in Paris a young, a very young wife. They came to Riond-Bosson on their honeymoon, which lasted exactly

IGNACE JAN PADEREWSKI

two weeks; at the end of that time she ordered her
trunks packed and left for Paris, telling her husband that he might follow or not, just as he chose.

The Count, being old, and doubtless loving with
as much intensity as his years permitted, returned
to Paris with a prompt docility. What the Countess
did after she got there, however, interests me far
more. Something entertaining, undoubtedly, for
life to a lady of her powers of decision held broad
possibilities.

Long afterward Madame Calvé, also, contributed
her temperamental mite to the history of Riond-
Bosson. Madame Guy d'Hardelot, composer of
songs, told it to me as engaging fragment of a time
when Calvé could make no journey except in her
society. Those journeys meant, according to the
composer, a constant unpacking of trunks for the
purpose of repacking them to go elsewhere.

Paderewski, admiring Calvé's exotic art, wished
to honor her when she reached Geneva, and insti-
tuted a dinner party at Riond-Bosson. The prima
donna accepted in ardent appreciation. She left
by boat to keep the appointment, but never fulfilled
it. The nearest she got to the spot was the quay at
Morges, where Paderewski had a carriage in waiting.
Madame d'Hardelot called attention to this polite
fact when the gang plank was lowered. But by that
time Calvé had changed her mind. She was not

dining that night, at least not at Villa Riond-Bosson. So she remained in her steamer chair while the boat took her back to Geneva.

My first visit to Paderewski's villa came in the height of his world successes, and when his Chopin playing renewed amorous longings in the gristly hearts of dowagers. Among the visitors there at that moment were Madame Wilkonska, his sister, whose face bore a strong resemblance to his in its firm yet gentle expression; Stojowski the composer, a piano pupil of Paderewski, and Monsignor Count Drobjowski.

The Monsignor, white-haired, noble-faced, and wearing a cassock with a jeweled cross at his breast, made a picturesque and commanding figure. His had been that life of self-abnegation for patriotism that has fallen to so many Poles. Taking part in an unsuccessful uprising he fled from Poland for his life, reaching Paris penniless. For a long time he served as omnibus driver in the French capital, finally taking orders in the church where he gained distinction.

His culture, his hard experiences, leaving a broad outlook, his brilliancy of mind made him a fascinating conversationalist. But in this aspect none approached Paderewski, at his best during dinner and when we gathered afterward on the moonlit terrace for our coffee. Those nights were unforgettable. The stillness under silver light; the lake softly glowing through branches of great trees; distant mountains against a dark blue sky, and the broad, splendid stone terrace in a flood of light from low French windows made the scene-setting for conversation in which Paderewski and Monsignor Drobjowski led.

The dining-room itself was a picture, moonlight streaming in through open windows to mingle with the shaded candle-glow. Down the long table a bed of pink geraniums or some other bright flowers were banked; from them radiated branches of roses. Mr. Paderewski sat opposite to me; his face in shadow, his hair, catching the light, standing out like an aureole of brass. Bridge sometimes followed our talks on the terrace, and lasted until three o'clock in the morning. On those nights Stojowski and I would steal up much earlier and softly to bed by way of the back stairs that we might not disturb the players.

Next the drawing-room was an apartment held sacred, not because of all the souvenirs of Paderewski's triumphs placed there, but on account of the mementos of his only son, by his first marriage, and then some years dead. The boy's wheeled-chair; his table at which he wrote, and all its furnishings were kept just as he left them, and every day fresh flowers were put there.

With the same curious fondness for noisy things
that distinguished Madame Patti, Paderewski had
seven parrots, and a big, white cockatoo, whose
screeches led the pandemonium until he was ban-
ished. Then the seven parrots left behind kept up
subdued mutterings, like a stranded opera chorus
whose prima donna had forsaken them. At Craig-
y-Nos the entire flock was of cockatoos, hung in gilt
cages in the conservatory, the commotion they made
being almost as bad as that of Patti's orchestrion.
Both musical celebrities had highly sensitive ears;
whistling set Paderewski wild, yet both harbored
those outlandish noises.

Only once at Riond-Bosson did I hear Paderewski
speak of music, except passingly; only once did he
play, when the proofs of his *Theme and Variations*
came from the publisher. Both my visits at Riond-
Bosson, however, were in midsummer; Paderewski
was resting, one hard musical season behind him,
and another ahead. In the course of that talk on
music, the great pianist said this, "Since Chopin,
Moritz Moszkowski best understands how to write
for the piano."

Knowing how this would please Moszkowski, I
told him of it one day. Curious to learn his methods
in writing things so pianistic, I asked him about
them. Moszkowski's first words told the secret, "I
compose at the piano. I know," he went on to say,

"that every composer prides himself on *not* writing
at the piano. But a painter must see a horse and
know how it is built in order to paint it. Of course,
in writing for orchestra I hear in my head the work
in its entirety.

"For that matter, I can compose in the street.
In driving from the railway station to my home, I
have composed a whole piano piece, and have talked
all the while. Yet afterward I try out every note
on the piano. I must play every note as I write that
I may see it in the hand. One reason why modern
composers write so badly for the piano is that they
compose away from the instrument instead of on
it."

My second stay at Riond-Bosson took on a more
intimate aspect, there being fewer visitors. It appeared, however, from the casual glimpse I got, that
Poles were present who did not dine at the family
table. Apparently another revolution had just failed
in their country. At such times more or less of them
fled to Riond-Bosson to find hearty welcome. It
was not only during the Great War that Paderewski
devoted his substance to patriotic purpose.

One day we went out to his farm, where Madame
Paderewska had gone on ahead to, herself, cook
luncheon. In a moment of absentmindedness, Mr.
Paderewski led me aboard an express at Morges,
instead of a local stopping near the farm. But

finally we reached it, after somewhat of a drive. There was nothing to regret, though, for our way lay between rare estates. One of these belonged to Madame Clicquot of endeared champagne memory; another was originally the property of Prince "Plon Plon" Bonaparte. On the fall of the Third Empire, he deeded it for safety to a trusted official of the court, deeded it so safely that he never got it back, for the court gentleman put it up at auction and the proceeds into his pocket.

On that drive the de Reszkes were brought into the conversation. During their earlier triumphs in America the three Poles had been closely intimate. Of poor Edouard, so big, so good-hearted, and who perished so miserably from privation during the war, he told an anecdote that was completely characteristic. The two brothers were then stopping, as was their custom in New York, at the Gilsey House. Coming in late after the opera performance, they were met by a party in the hotel lobby. As all seemed to know them, Jean, ignorant of even their names, talked ahead with the tact that distinguished him. Not so Edouard, however. In deep thought and utterly silent he stood there towering above the rest. Suddenly in the midst of things, light dawned on him; he had remembered their names. "How do you do!" he roared abruptly with a bass heartiness that set the chandeliers to tinkling, "How do you do!" and he shook hands all around as though he had just met them.

The farm-house we caught sight of finally; a big oak tree sheltered it; wistaria blossoms and the glossy leaves of an espaliered pear trailed against its white walls. Mr. Paderewski loved the rambling simplicity of the place better than the stateliness of Riond-Bosson. "Never a thing shall be touched here," he said fondly. "It shall be like a dear, untroubled face that I shall always have to return to, no matter where my journeyings may lead me.

"Those big trees, now beyond the property line, must be mine; otherwise the owner will fell them for timber. Knowing that I am an artist, he asks thousands of francs more than he should. But knowing that I am an artist, he is also certain that I will pay it.

"People strangely think that an artist's money comes easily, that he does not have to work for it. They forget that he is productive only for fifteen years, and that the foundation of it all is long preceding years of drudgery. Most of us have a tendency to overlook the fact that a little while ahead we can no longer earn big sums, and we give on, spend on, as if it were to last for always; as if to-morrow would be just as good as to-day."

The mood was prophetic. Like the rest of those artists of whom he spoke, Mr. Paderewski has gone on giving and spending. But to what noble purpose. For Poland and his countrymen he has sacrificed almost all that he possessed, and for which he toiled prodigiously. He gave up, too, his great earning powers as pianist in order to dedicate his whole life to the cause. Artists, some of them, have a strain of nobility surpassing that of kings. Paderewski is one of the noblest among them all. For proper measure of gratitude he will have to wait; perhaps death and history will bring it.

What followed that day in the conversation touched on this very theme of gratitude. His sentiments then may have aided him philosophically later. "The gratitude of those we do for! I hate the word!" he exclaimed. "The man to whom we do a favor recognizes his inferiority and it rankles. A favor is often the poison of friendship. There are some who have an exaggerated feeling of gratitude; that is an unfortunate trait. I have it. I want to repay a kindness a hundred times. And I have done it.

"There was a man, poor fellow he is dead now, who once did me a kindness when I needed it. At a banquet given me in Poland he was present. In my speech I told of his act, but I added, 'I do not hold it against him,' and I think he understood what I meant."

After years of that drudgery of preparation of

which Paderewski spoke, and in hard poverty, before that gold which he gave out so royally began
to pour in, he was in London. His first manager
there was Daniel Mayer. He told me the story.
This line in a Vienna newspaper led to Mayer's interest in the pianist: "The only artist, aside from
Stavenhagen and d'Albert, who knows how to hold
his public is Paderewski." It was in March of that
year that Mr. Arthur Chappell, the music publisher,
and one whose influence made him a power, said to
the manager, "What do you think of the cheek of
this youngster? He writes to ask if I will arrange
four concerts for him in London."

"What is his name?" queried Mayer, whose experience had been that all great artists had, at one
time or another, to be youngsters.

"Paderewski or something like it. I can't read
it," returned the impatient Chappell, and gave
Mayer the letter.

The outcome was that Paderewski arrived in London for his four concerts. Briefly, as Mayer described him, he was then very slim and very long-
haired. The first concert in the series attracted but
a small audience. To Mayer it brought the assurance of Paderewski's great art. "You will have
London at your feet," he said to the pianist.

"Go away, flatterer," was all the answer he got.

The next morning after the concert the *Daily*

Telegraph stated, "The lion of the season is I. J. Paderewski," who, when he saw it, said, "Am I then out of a menagerie?" With each succeeding appearance receipts grew. The fourth, a Chopin recital, was sold out. Going to tell him the news, Mayer found Paderewski in a gloomy little corner at the piano rooms practising. Moved to tears on hearing the good tidings, he put his face in his hands, bowing his head against the key board. "It's wrong; I can't take their money!" he said brokenly, adding suddenly, "I can't play at all!" But he did play, and the assurance was that he played superbly.

Prior to that Paderewski had concertized with astounding success in Paris. At his début there, he told me, tremendous applause interrupted his opening group, and he thought to himself, "What will it be when the end comes?" But when the end did come, there was nothing. Presently he learned the custom of the French, all in the moment of performance, little, perhaps nothing, when that performance is concluded.

Berlin gave Paderewski no such welcome as did Paris, London, and New York. And Berlin he consistently loathed. It was no more possible for him to like the Prussians than for them to like him. A people that had allowed the tremendous and emotional in Bach to become militarized in its interpretation, was unlikely to find joy in the imaginative, poetic qualities of Paderewski's playing.   Hence, mutual antipathy.

Personally, I do not doubt when, during the World War, Paderewski recruited and equipped by his own effort a Polish regiment to go to the front, that there must have come to him an added satisfaction in the knowledge that Berliners would, perhaps, get a share of its bullets.   Even heroes are human.

Paderewski is complex; he is also very nervous. As I mainly knew him, he was gentle, absolutely simple, lacking egotism, frankly honest.   Also I got a glimpse of the tricks that irritating things played on his nerves, tensely strained from years of tremendous practising and playing.   At such times his mood changed suddenly to one of self-centered unreasonableness.

This trait of nerves, inseparable from the great artist, doubtless made his task as Poland's Premier difficult, wellnigh impossible.   The direct straightforwardness of his nature was never fitted to cope with the double-dealing distinguishing diplomacy. Neither could the exquisite inborn tact that he possessed prove inexhaustible under nervous strain. With his sensitive soul absorbed in the cause of Poland, the situation became more acute.

About him as Poland's Premier were factions less far-seeing than he, but equally determined;

facing him before the Peace Conference and in the League of Nations was the self-interest of the Entente Allies, each self-seeking, each greedy for advantage. On the other hand were Poland's demands, often inordinate. What Paderewski suffered in this complex situation can be only faintly surmised.

Therefore, and to musicians especially, his admirable measure of success, in circumstances as difficult as the world has ever offered, should be a matter of inveterate pride. Very poor in his boyhood, he had risen as musician to the heights of world celebrity. That in itself made romance sufficient for any life. As pianist, his dignity, his self-respect, his scrupulous integrity, had won him high regard as a world figure. The nations of the Entente Allies, trusting him implicitly, welcomed him at the Peace Conference and at the League of Nations; his people called him to the post of Premier for those same reasons.

Of Paderewski's absolute devotion to his country's cause, there can be no doubt. He has sacrificed everything to it, a world career as artist, a fortune, his present and his future. In a critical juncture his efforts went far toward bridging a gap otherwise impassable; the single one among his people who could have achieved it. In the history of Poland Ignace Jan Paderewski will live immortal; in the

history of world musicians he will occupy a niche
alone.

But it is to those days of peace, before the world
was set in conflagration, that it is happier to turn
in mention of Paderewski.   The calm life of Riond-
Bosson was charming, but the supreme quiet of his
farm made a still better framing for his gentle nature.   Every man trudging nearby roads knew and
greeted him deferentially with the sturdy self-
respect that the Swiss drink in with their air; not the
Swiss as we know them, contaminated by life in
foreign hostelries, but the home-bred, home-loving
Swiss, the truest, sturdiest, equal-rights democrats
with the simplest form of republic that the world
holds.

That day, while we were eating the luncheon
which Madame Paderewska had cooked for us, a
little goat sprang into the room.   At the doorway
by which he had entered two children's faces smiled.
The same old ruse that the rest of us once practised,
an excuse, any excuse to get into a loved presence.
The goat, quite willing to be made an apology for
his owners, walked up to Mr. Paderewski and took
as custom the lettuce leaves fed to him.

With exclamations of delighted surprise, as if
the goat had never eaten before, the small con-
spirators tumbled in; they were in their best clothes,
their faces shone from soap and water.   Once inside,

their shyness vanished. Both were telling Paderewski the goat's latest adventures. Madame Paderewska and me they looked upon as grown-up people, to be answered in monosyllables and with forced politeness. But Paderewski was regarded as one of themselves, sufficiently youthful and interesting to be taken as an equal. Until tea time, they and the goat tagged after him, and then all three went to bed, perhaps together.

It was during tea that Madame Paderewska asked the hour. "Six o'clock, and we have missed the last train until nine," her husband answered.

"With guests at Riond-Bosson!" she cried excitedly. "And we cannot telephone them to have dinner served at eight. What shall we do?"

"Take the nine o'clock train, without fail," said Paderewski smiling. Handing me the strawberry tarts he went on jovially, "Help yourself, we still have four hours until dinner."

And we had. It was past ten when we entered the hall at Riond-Bosson, where the guests later declared the idea had come to them to meet us in their night clothes as appropriate to our late arrival. Twelve o'clock struck before we arose from the table and went out on the terrace for coffee.

It is well that there is no gift of prophecy to foretell life. Much of honor and distinction, much of battling turmoil and of harrowing anguish have come since then to Paderewski. My happiest recollections of him must remain of that day.

In our last moments at the farm the call of a cuckoo came from the wood in the still of growing night; the blue Alps, pink at their snow-covered crests, were outlined mistily against a purple sky; green trees dotted the fields of yellowing wheat; there was a scent of dew and flowers in the air. For some minutes Mr. Paderewski stood drinking it all in, then, sighing, turned to go.

Perhaps, some day, unchanged at heart after troubled years, I shall find him again in the place he described as a dear, unchanging face awaiting him at every journey's end.

CHAPTER VII

MARY GARDEN

MARY GARDEN'S career has been spectacularly brilliant. Taking fate into her own hands, she bent it to her will; hers is the type that rules. To Paris she went a stranger; without a single mis-step she mounted upward steadily until, a foreigner without connections or influence, she had conquered.

With commanding successes behind her, Miss Garden returned to America as the greatest exponent of modern French opera yet seen here. After twenty-one years on the stage, she also ruled as Artistic Director of the Chicago Opera Company, ranking next in importance to the Metropolitan.

It was in the earlier days of Miss Garden's career at the Opéra Comique that I first learned to know her. At that time she lived in a little apartment in the Rue Washington, where her drawing-room was furnished in the style of the First Empire, with a wonderful carved head from Bruges of John the Baptist hung against the wall as a kind of spiritual *entrée*.

And oh, the courage of her! She had already travelled far in the five years that she had been before the public. In the Paris art world she loomed big. Madame Marchesi in speaking of her at that period, said, "Of the Americans singing at the Comique she is the greatest." And Madame Marchesi, it will be recalled, was not Mary Garden's teacher, but she was the teacher of two celebrities preceding her at the Comique, Sybil Sanderson, for whom Massenet composed *Esclarmonde*, and Emma Nevada. Poor, beautiful Sybil Sanderson of whom that same Madame Marchesi said, "She took her career in both hands and threw it out of the window." While this tragedy was in progress, it is well to recall that Mary Garden unselfishly proved a loyal friend to her when it meant sacrifice. And up to the end, Miss Garden maintained that loyalty.

She was among the few present at the once fêted American's funeral, a funeral at which Massenet, who in her fair youth had gone distracted over her, was not in attendance, nor did he trouble himself to send flowers. But Massenet had so many loves that, had they died, to have provided flowers for the funerals of all would have bankrupted him. He was still in love when I met him, that time with a contralto for whom he composed *Ariadne*. And he was so old that he had to wear a skull-cap and shawl to help keep out the chill of May weather. The situation was as thoroughly French as is his music.

After Miss Garden's New York triumphs in his *Thaïs* and *Jongleur*, I said to her, "Massenet should be grateful to you for doing for him what none other could do in America."

"He has not said so," she answered. Then smiling demurely, added, "but he has never sent me notes and photographs as he did all the rest; so, perhaps, he does regard me differently."

Miss Garden was always spoken of in Paris as an American; when she came to the Manhattan Opera House she was accredited this country as homeland from her babyhood, perhaps for advertising purposes. In reality she was eleven years old when she left her birthplace, Aberdeen, to set sail for America. And Scotch she has remained ever since.

Few people are more musical in their instinct for melody than are the Scotch; no people, excepting the Armenians, are so keenly practical. Possessing eminently the latter trait, it is doubtful if Miss Garden indulged at any time in day dreams. As a child, she invented little plays and acted in them, invariably the leading rôle; in girlhood she sang in a Chicago church choir.

That she should gravitate to Paris was the only natural thing to be expected. She seems intuitively to have known the right course to take; Paris was the sole city in the world fitted to develop her peculiar type of gifts. "But I waited until I got there to see what *was* to be done before I decided to *do* it," was the canny way she put it on that afternoon of our first meeting, as she sat enthroned on her Empire sofa.

Her figure was girlishly beautiful, her profile that of a statue. Valuable as these assets were, the generals that best helped her win her battles were grit and intelligence. "I like to fight," she once declared, "battles never frighten me." And one may add of her quite candidly, nor does anything else.

Many having voices superior to Miss Garden's in its palmy days have failed remotely to arrive. Miss Garden, however, sings a rôle not with her voice alone, but with her whole being. In a characterization, hers is the ability to catch the subtle essence that is French. To Anglo-Saxons, Wagner's music dramas are clearly comprehensible, and in them they have given noble portrayals; in French modern opera that elusive something, failing which an impersonation becomes as a lamp lacking oil, is persistently missing. This elusive something is Miss Garden's mental property; she lives it.

Her art in acting is exquisitely finished and it is commanding; she can be sophisticated to a degree that is ultra-French; she can display equally, as in *Jongleur*, that supreme simplicity which, like a tongue of fire, touches the foreheads of only the genuinely great.

In Paris Miss Garden's first act was to shut herself out from all that was not French. In a quiet home, with three generations of Parisian inmates, she studied French under the trees in a high-walled garden. When she had become sufficiently acquainted with the vernacular, she emerged. To seven vocal teachers she went in a city that possibly has seven hundred of them, mostly bad ones, before she found the large per cent. of two whom she could trust, Faugére of the Opéra Comique and Chevalier.

The Paris Opéra, then and now one of the worst existing travesties, could afford her no inspiration. At the Opéra Comique the situation proved quite other. Carré, of splendid artistic tastes, was its director. There she found the one field not only for a guiding of her talent, but for displaying it.

It was a very happy accident that prevented Miss Garden's début in the innocuous rôle of *Michaela* in *Carmen* and gave her, instead, as first chance the heroine in Charpentier's *Louise*, destined to be one of her best successes. Of that night all doubtless know that Miss Garden came to the theatre as an auditor; replaced a prima donna fallen ill, and from the third act on sang out the performance. It was quite characteristic of her to stake all on a single turn, and, never nervous once she knows a part, probably Miss Garden, herself, was less surprised at the outcome than were her hearers.

The confidence she appears to have felt that night came without rehearsal of any sort. She had not even the advantage of familiarity with the piano accompaniment. The woman in whose house she stopped being ill and unable to stand the sound of an instrument, Mary Garden had memorized *Louise's* music as she tapped time with her foot against the floor. Her public interpretation of the rôle brought her two hundred and five appearances in it at the Opéra Comique.

When Miss Garden's monthly fee for singing in opera was but a tithe of the sum later paid her nightly, she knew how to make a home and make it beautiful. With Scotch thrift she had gone shopping in out of the way corners or picked up bargains on her travels. Each article appeared to have a history connected with it. There was a bust of Voltaire, found after a day's search in the Latin Quarter; there was a marble statue that she had bought in Italy for twenty dollars, and so the inventory went.

Following her American successes, which greatly increased her means, she forsook the Rue Washington for the Avenue Malakoff. But no prima donna ideas of extravagance attacked Miss Garden. Being Scotch, she and thrift remained intimates. She audited her household accounts as carefully as if she were still in Aberdeen. *Thaïs* and *Mélisande* could not have accomplished this; she could be *Thaïs* and *Mélisande* and still remain Mary Garden.

In Paris, while Miss Garden was making a tremendous success as *Aphrodite*, she had invited me to come to her dressing-room one night between the acts. After the first and second, I decided to wait, thinking a more elaborate toilette might demand attention for the third. But it did not. The part of wisdom seemed to be to go at once.

Before her mirror Miss Garden stood giving a final touch. Her maid had been dismissed to make room for visitors, three besides myself. On one of the two chairs sat a very sophisticated old Frenchman; on the other was an American woman whose spouse stood beside her.

"You can get this for drawing-room use," the prima donna was advising as I entered, and continued applying a milky liquid to her arms. The American, wife, home, country, all forgot, was gazing spellbound and with popping eyes at the length of two perfect arms being turned to marble. His wife, disregarding all those kind directions of how to get and use things, plainly expressed in a steely glare, *"This* is Paris!" And Miss Garden? She was demurely smiling, enjoying a situation that she had created.

To Mr. Armstrong
with my best
compliments
Mary Garden
Aphrodite.

1906

MARY GARDEN AS APHRODITE

During those seven years of her Paris successes, though regarded as an American, little, very little, had been printed about Miss Garden in our newspapers; in the magazines, nothing. Filled with enthusiasm for her *Aphrodite*, I wrote an article about her. For sixteen months it travelled from one New York magazine to another, but it was not considered "timely." Just prior to her arrival in this country it was published; the first magazine article on Mary Garden to be printed in America.

When Miss Garden made her début at the Manhattan Opera House, her task became a double one; to triumph for herself and to triumph for contemporary French opera. Up to that time American audiences had but slight acquaintance with modern French opera composers. And, lacking a great leading woman, the few presented had gained scant recognition. Even Jean de Reszke could not win approval for Massenet's *Le Cid* and *Werther*. Other spasmodic, intermittent attempts to give modern French opera failed, and signally.

The granting of the Legion of Honor to Mary Garden by the French Government in 1921 was belated. She had won it through her French impersonations by the close of her first New York season.

As a singing actress she swept the town and with her the hitherto rejected opera of France sprang into favor. Very splendidly has she repaid the nation whose appreciative encouragement started her a long way forward toward her world success.

From the moment that she stepped ashore in this country, Miss Garden's personality spread her fame automatically. To the newspapermen, the most difficult, yet the easiest class to interest, she proved a bonanza. Her only artistic peers in this line have been Sara Bernhardt and Emma Calvé.

Invariably Miss Garden was awaited at the pier on each return as bringing something startling which would make good copy. Once as she sailed up the bay that something failed to materialize. "What *shall* I say to them!" was her racking thought. The first reporter whom she met solved the problem. Spying the ridge made under her glove by a ring on the third finger of her left hand, he asked breathlessly, "What is this?" By that time reporters stood ten deep about her. "You men find out everything," was her only comment. That settled it; she was engaged; the more imaginative ones gave her a Turk or a prince as fiancé.

Mary Garden's immediate acceptance by New York had its influence upon Paris audiences. Had she failed, they might not have appreciated her less, but, succeeding, they appreciated her more. When she appeared as *Salome*, and in an intermission between New York engagements, the receipts were the largest in the history of the Paris Opéra.

She learned the rôle against her friends' advice. "They thought," said Miss Garden, "that I could not do it." Adding curtly, "But I did." In one aspect of the portrayal she was more keenly far-seeing than was Richard Strauss, who thought it impossible for her to sing the rôle and also do the dance.

"If I cannot dance, I shall not sing it," was her fiat. Then she explained to him something which he, apparently, had not realized. The first part of the opera was hideously difficult vocally and in every way; the second did not make such tremen· dous demands. The reserve strength equal to the first half of the work would sustain the second and the dance.

At the time when all Paris rushed to see *Salome* I met Max Nordau, to whom Moritz Moszkowski, his close friend, had introduced me. Nordau we well know through his book *Degeneration*. One of the keenest contemporary minds and one of the most absolutely fearless of beings, what he had to say apropos of Richard Strauss was pertinent; it is just as pertinent still. He had been speaking of modern composers and the choice of grotesque librettos by some, when he said this:

There is the Young Italian School; of course, the Italians are bright, mettlesome people, loving striking, dramatic, intense situations, but not one of them of whom I know has chosen a sickly, morbid subject; Puccini, for instance, has never made any such choice. But there are the German degenerates who have that sickly, morbid fancy, like Richard Strauss, who as a neurotic composer has chosen the libretto of *Elektra*, by von Hofmannsthal, a neurotic writer. With both it is a question of diseased nerves. In the first place Strauss chooses *Salome*, bad sickly, foul, unnatural, a morbid subject, by that poor man Wilde. Then he turns to von Hofmannsthal, who, in his *Elektra*, takes a healthy subject and contaminates it, covers it with a highfalutin verbosity, paints over it a framework of abominably abused classical poetry, tears asunder beautiful lines and innoculates them with modern disease.

"Is the taste of the public to blame?" The public has no taste! It is impressed by its natural leaders. It flocks to hear the last and 'most beautiful creation of modern art.' Few have the courage to say: 'I have seen it, and feel only nauseated.' Fifty per cent. will say, perhaps: 'I am not sufficiently informed to decide.' Fifty per cent, the snobs, the yellow-plushes, the less they like it, the more repulsive they find it, the more loudly will they acclaim its beauty. They are attitudinizing.

Good music breaks forth from the heart and the soul; it is not a something that can be sucked from the fingers. The dearth of great composers is due alone to the fact that they have no inspiration. We have perfect technicians, but they have no heart, no life, no feeling, no soul; they have only ambition, vanity, and greed. Richard Strauss never invented one well-defined melody, and if one occurs in his compositions, it is always a borrowed popular one.

Did Oscar Hammerstein appreciate Mary Garden, who made a world fame for his opera house? In a way, perhaps, but it was a way peculiarly his own. Toward the end of his career at the Manhattan, and finding himself in desperate straits, Miss Garden made herculean efforts to save him. Five nights in succession she would sing in performances divided between New York and Philadelphia. At that juncture, Mr. Hammerstein started suit against his faithful artist for excess fees he claimed to have paid her by settling in dollars instead of in francs.

With the passing of the Manhattan Opera House, Miss Garden passed to Chicago and beyond my ken. In that city, as Artistic Director of the opera, Mary Garden founded for herself an Arc de Triomphe, on which, like her hero, the great Napoleon, to inscribe her battles.

CHAPTER VIII

ENRICO CARUSO AND JOHN McCORMACK

THE spell of Caruso's voice has carried to the confines of civilization and beyond them. In the jungles of Africa and in the foothills of the Himalayas; in Alaska and on our prairies, the records have made it familiar. His was the singing romance of a universal celebrity.

The first time I heard him was as *Rhadames* to the *Aïda* of Madame Nordica, and at Covent Garden the summer before he came to America. Something engaging happened that night, which I always connect with the performance. Miss Zélie de Lussan, no doubt still remembered as a charming *Carmen*, and Mr. Loudon Charlton, at that time managing Madame Nordica, were of our party of three. Looking radiantly beautiful, Miss de Lussan was arranging herself well to the front of the box, perhaps to save people the bother of craning their necks to get a good view of her, when Charlton exclaimed, "I remember that stunning gown of yours! You wore it two years ago." Then settled complacently back, as a man should after such a feat of memory.

Caruso's voice on that first hearing struck me more
forcibly than did any qualities back of it, nor were
his tones flung out with the prodigal plenitude displayed in years following. And memories of splendid climaxes, made by Tamagno in *Trovatore* and
in *Otello*, still lingered. Not to have recalled them
would have been an injustice to the older tenor, for
in *De Quella Pira* Tamagno had not been equalled
by any to whom I had listened, and his *Otello* was
of an eloquence vocally and histrionically that has,
I fancy, never been approached by another since the
music was written. Alone his high G sharps, A and
B, for instance, given on the first entrance, were like
a flash of lightning through black darkness. With
these things I have mentioned, Tamagno's story of
conquest seemed to end. Nevertheless, to have done
them as he did made commanding achievement.

When his electrical high notes came, no prima
donna except Madame Nordica could keep him
away from the footlights. "How do you manage
it?" I asked her.

"By grabbing him and constantly saying, 'Look
at me! Look at me! Look at me!'"

There were moments, though, when he forgot this
footlight habit. The last act of *Otello* worked him
into a frenzy that swept his audience with him.
One night at Covent Garden with Madame Eames
as *Desdemona*, and a lovely *Desdemona* she was, for

the heart-breaking calm of the part suited her
temperament, Tamagno grew unusually violent.
Smashing the bed on which he was strangling her,
prima donna, tenor, and bed all came down together.

If Tamagno were to-day alive, people would
rush to see and hear his *Otello*. Audiences change.
The Italian came here too near to the day of Jean
de Reszke, the finished eloquence of his art, and his
small voice with which he did big things. They
had become used to one type of tenor, and worshipped that type exclusively. Had Caruso instead
of Tamagno sung to that generation of opera-goers,
people would have wagged their heads and said
sadly, "Ah, but he hasn't Jean's finish." But
Caruso had something which Jean had not.

Tamagno with his robustness, a robustness often
raw but with flashing top notes, was followed by
Caruso with his richer, mellower, more vital charm
of tone, which never reached the level of Jean's
in finished delivery. But by that time audiences
were ready to accept that something which Jean had
not.

As Caruso's voice steadily gained in volume, volume became the vocal fashion. To achieve it, and
without Caruso's phenomenal powers, some valuable
voices were forced to the point that their owners
could no longer use them.

When the beloved de Reszke departed this life

ENRICO CARUSO

This photograph was made at Covent Garden Opera, London, shortly
before Caruso left for New York to make his début at the
Metropolitan.

vocally, many heads were shaken mournfully, many tongues said, "We'll never have another Jean." Not by that name, no. But another of somewhat the same style seems to be here. This time he is called Muratore.

Some day, perhaps a few years hence, when a new generation of opera-goers has arisen, there may doubtless come a robust tenor with brains, who will sing all the way from *Manrico* to *Tristan*. Then he will be pattern for all tenors and the idol of all audiences. The greatness of Caruso's name, however, will linger undimmed with that generation, just as Jean de Reszke's remained undimmed with an older one. But to that newer generation de Reszke and Caruso will mean but names, exactly as Mario lives in name only with us, though our grandfathers remembered him differently, having heard him. That is the history of opera. It is also, in great measure, the history of all human life. If this were not so, there would be no to-morrows, no hope, no upspringing romance, only yesterdays to remember, and life itself would be done.

The autumn following Caruso's Covent Garden season in which I heard him, he made his début at the Metropolitan, where he was destined to grow and grow immeasurably in his voice and in his art. The aristocratic distinction demanded in a number of his rôles he never satisfactorily visualized;

neither in height nor figure did he sustain romantic ideals. But the glory of his voice made his audiences forget all else.

On his début night as the *Duke* in *Rigoletto*, he appeared terribly nervous. Madame Helen Mapleson as the *Countess* had her fan crushed by him in the first act, as he clutched at her arm. He must have recalled his sensations with some amusement for he drew a capital caricature of them as *Duke* and *Countess*, and colored it into the bargain. Madame Mapleson's husband, Lionel, treasures it still. As a whole, though, that *Rigoletto* performance was far from brilliant. At his next appearance, Caruso's abandon increased decidedly. On the first night, however, no marked proclamation was given that a new tenor had come who would reign absolute at the Metropolitan for the rest of his life.

Twice I met Enrico Caruso when my writing took me to see him. Aside from that purpose I did not feel special impulse to seek him out, for there was something in his personality that did not appeal to me. This by no means prevented me from seeing and valuing fine traits that placed him high among artists.

The first call upon him was made at Hotel York, in Seventh Avenue, where he stopped in his early days here. He was genial, he was interested; no boy could have shown greater simplicity or more ready desire to prove agreeable. Struggling with English then, which he spoke fluently later, he told me among other things, and quite earnestly, "As a boy I sing on a church." It seemed to amuse him to amuse others, and through genuine kindness of heart.

The second time that I met him was behind the scenes at the Metropolitan, on a night when he was singing *Rhadames*. Ready for the first act, he talked to me in his dressing-room, and we passed together down the stairs, he on his way to the stage. I have read and heard much of the nervousness that assailed Caruso before singing in opera. That night, at least, there seemed no trace of it, but, instead, recurring moments of abstraction showing concentration on the performance ahead.

He would be talking and suddenly break off, stopping quite still on a step of the stairs to emit a tone *forte*. Then, apparently satisfied that his voice was all right, he would resume the conversation. I am quite sure, though, that thought of his voice never left him during our talk. It was intense anxiety about his singing, but it was not nervousness as the term is accepted.

And his dressing-room! In those days it was his fantastic, almost freakish idea that bad luck would attend his stage performance unless certain objects were on his dressing-table. There were strange looking dolls, some grown quite disreputable through much handling, and between these were put little pictures of sacred subjects, the whole placed quite haphazard like a rummage sale. Every item of the outfit had some special story connected with the supernatural or good luck powers ascribed to it. On those days when Caruso sang, his valet would bring the collection in a cab to the Metropolitan and put it in place. Later on, I have heard, this custom was not so generally followed.

One night in that same dressing-room, Caruso got into an argument. He had asserted with positiveness that a singer's name carried more weight than did his voice. If the king of tenor voices had not been a modest one, he would have failed to dabble in any such subject. Others about him that evening disagreed hotly. "Wait, I'll prove it," said Caruso, and left the room.

They were giving *Pagliacci* that night. Albert Reiss, whose voice was still smaller than the small rôles that he sang, was doing the *Harlequin*, allotted a *Serenade* to sing behind the scenes. Caruso found Reiss, who without much coaxing gave up the *Serenade* to his noted colleague. When its music came in the orchestra, Caruso sang, giving his best. After it ended not a ripple of applause stirred in the audience. Neither, apparently, had any of the critics noticed it, for no line in the newspapers next morning mentioned a sudden improvement in "Reiss."

The story was told me by Christopher Campanari, son of Giuseppe Campanari the baritone, and who was present in Caruso's dressing-room during the incident. One bright spot remained in this conclusive arraignment, and that was that no success had blinded Caruso as to what carried most with the multitude, and also with many who did not consider themselves as belonging to the multitude at all.

Had Caruso been less staunchly loyal to the Metropolitan, and more grasping for the amassing of wealth, he would have headed his own opera company and reaped a golden harvest far larger than that which eventually fell to him, though his earning powers were tremendous as things existed.

When the tenor returned from Mexico where he had given a limited number of performances, Amato told me, "Caruso says that the seventy thousand dollars he brought back with him will go to pay his taxes." In this connection it must be recalled that a large proportion of his gross income came from the royalties on his records.

A great charm in the noted tenor's romance was that he carried unimpaired throughout singing triumphs his modesty, his loyalty, and his generosity. Those traits combined to make him beloved by his colleagues from the humblest among them. As

Charles Hackett, the American tenor, once told me, "Caruso never dictated who should sing with him. Always ready to keep peace in the operatic family, he would sometimes say, 'I know that their voices are not all they should be. But, come on, children, we'll do our best.'"

Affectionate tradition of him at that opera house says further that never once did he cause trouble; always letter perfect in his rôles, though playing pranks in rehearsals, as he loved to do, he would fall soberly into his part when his cue came; no call boy was needed to summon him in a performance, five minutes before time for his entrance he was ready and waiting in the wings. These are virtues, though not all of them virtues invariably practised by tenors.

Many apocryphal anecdotes have doubtless been attached to Caruso, his whimsical unexpectedness lent credence to almost any, however fantastic. To meet him with insight was to know that certain fine traits marked him, traits I have mentioned, which endeared him strongly to his colleagues, and which will grace his memory. Caruso lived the splendidly triumphant romance of his voice with a simple, naïve mind, and a generous heart.

The big heart back of his songs, equally with his singing of them, has made John McCormack a popular idol to American audiences. No other tenor is given such genuine affection by such tremendous following. His is the singing romance of a king of the old Irish minstrels reincarnated.

In the days when McCormack was appearing at the Manhattan Opera House, he gave me a glimpse of the picturesque beginnings of that romance of his, a romance which has since extended to all points on the map of our land that he now calls his own. He was at that time just starting to sing his way into people's hearts with *Snowy Breasted Pearl* and like melodies of his native Ireland.

John McCormack's father of County Athlone seems to have had a fixed idea that the discipline of the school bench was far superior to any provided in the home circle. Having no very large initiative at the age of three, John submitted. Unsteady of leg as such young legs will be, he was trotted next door to the Marists' Monastery to imbibe learning. In reality the step he was taking was as momentous as *Siegfried's* quest of the dragon; in both cases it led to a future as popular tenor.

When the boy made his way into the school-room that morning, with his big Irish eyes and a brogue quite as winning, he appears at the same time to have walked straight into the heart of Brother Hugh, a musician. To John McCormack, Brother

Hugh proved what might be termed an honorary musical mother.

There were forenoons of Latin, and afternoons of History, perhaps mainly Irish; in between them was singing. Whether sacred or secular doubtless mattered little to John, both allowing self-expression in melodious noise. His pipings caught the quick ear of Brother Hugh, and in the first year in learning what discipline meant, probably before the boy knew what they called it, he was trained in *do, re, mi.*

With passage of time, he grew in knowledge of the old Gregorian music, and of Irish folk songs which are, so many of them, very near themselves to being sacred music. Then came his first public appearance. He was seven years old when he made it. Their Bishop had come to visit the Marists. As part of the welcome, John was put on a table to sing before his lordship. The selection was *Absence Makes the Heart Grow Fonder;* one perhaps not exactly clerical in its sentiment.

It is easy to picture Brother Hugh as standing modestly in the background, too intimately associated with the day's vocal glory to do otherwise, while his Bishop commended the future tenor and gave him a penny. His first fee. "After getting it," McCormack told me, "it really didn't matter what he said."

JOHN McCORMACK

Seven years in all McCormack studied with the Marists, which made his age ten when he left them. And in those years, as he said, he had acquired his entire vocal training, aside from a few suggestions given him later in Italy by Maestro Savona. In those early years, too, he was thoroughly founded in Latin, which his natural tendency was to pronounce as Italian.

Life in the open, with the fresh green about him, and the River Shannon seem to have made up the rest of his boyhood. Of the river itself he told me, "Tradition said that it was full of fish. I have sat all night on its banks and caught only rain. If the night was fine, I caught nothing at all."

His life in the open, and that "discipline" early afforded by his father, left indelible impression on McCormack's manhood. As he seemed to me when I first met him, he has no doubt seemed ever since to those who know him, the most unsophisticated of tenors in his genuine boyishness, accepting the world as a good place to live in if only he honestly pleases it.

In view of all that has since come to McCormack, his first nights in opera, which were in Italy, must seem to him like a humorous dream. Chance for a try out at Sante Croce was offered, and he took it. On big maps the place is indicated by a dot placed near Florence, small maps have no room for that dot at all. Its population was at the time of which he spoke four hundred. It is surely that still. Its opera house was a kind of family foyer; its public extremely critical. Good tones moved them to fiery fervor, bad ones to malediction.

Several performances were sung by McCormack successfully. Then came a night when he was cast as *Faust* in the Italian version of Gounod's opera. In his dressing-room, for some reason, perhaps imaginary, the tenor began to worry about a high B. It would not come until well on in the opera, so ample time was still left him to worry about it. The more he thought of it, the more scared he grew. Seized with uncontrollable terror in the instant that that the high B was due, he turned and ran off the stage. Without knowing why, the chorus ran after him. The orchestra, what there was of it, stopped still.

There sat Sante Croce's inhabitants, for they had come in a body; the house was quite full, the stage quite empty. Fortunately for McCormack and his choral followers, the audience was too mystified to instantly start a commotion. Explanations pretty soon filtered through from behind the scenes, which at Sante Croce was very near to the front row of seats. Quickly those explanations reached the last standee. Then a burst of applause shook candles loose from their sockets. All understood the situation completely; not one there would have done other than had he. Gradually heartened by the uproar, John McCormack returned to sing to its makers, bringing his high B along.

We should never have heard many a distinguished foreign-born opera singer had it not been for the small opera houses of Italy and Germany, where natives of those two musical countries receive a part, and often the best part of their training.

Pasquale Amato frequently talked to me on this very subject of small opera houses, and for America. His own early training was made in the little opera houses of southern Italy; he knew the worth of them. Amato travelled here extensively; he travelled with insight; he knew our musical needs.

The subsidizing of opera houses by the municipalities, as it is followed in Italy, would with us be impossible. Amato evolved another plan for giving opera in American cities as generally as it is given in Italy. To me his plan seemed practicable, and it was this: Have a chorus of local singers trained in the opera selected; give the smaller rôles to local church-choir singers or to young vocal students desiring to work their way upward; engage professionals for the principal rôles, and on the easier terms that performances in a chain of cities would warrant. He felt that local managers would gladly consent to let their theatres to such organizations on the same basis as that granted to dramatic companies.

Amusingly small as the Sante Croce beginning may seem, considering what the future held in store for McCormack, there have been beginnings still smaller. Gianoli-Galletti, who also sang at the Manhattan Opera House, had one of them. A capital *buffo* in his day, and genuinely prized in Italy where *buffos* are more valued than they are here, his début brought him a short engagement.

It took him a two hours' drive from the nearest railway station to reach it. On arriving, he started out with professional instinct to look for the opera house. But he found none.

"Where is the opera house?" he asked of a lounger.

"It hasn't come yet," was the answer.

"Not come yet?" he echoed blankly.

"No, it will get here to-morrow," calmly returned his informant.

Then Gianoli-Galletti discovered that he was to sing in opera in a tent.

CHAPTER IX

FRIEDA HEMPEL

IN the days when as a boy I studied music in Germany, there was at Baden-Baden a prima donna called Biancha Bianchi, whose real name was Schwartz. In that charming little town they adored her. When she drove to the opera house to sing *Marie* in *The Daughter of the Regiment*, her drum strapped atop the big basket containing her costumes, she passed between an avenue of smiling faces clear up to the stage door.

Her fame spread to Vienna, where she was asked to sing *Sonnambula* and the rest of her repertory at the Imperial Opera. Getting as far as that building, she turned around and went home to Baden-Baden, too scared to sing. It took several years to coax her back. After she finally sang there, however, the Viennese adored her exactly as she had been adored at Baden-Baden.

Bianchi's beauty of voice, her audacious assurance in all that went to make a coloratura, had surely never within many years been equalled by any in Germany, until Frieda Hempel of Leipsic arrived with a suave, velvety loveliness of tone in sustained melodies greater than was Bianchi's. Psychologically there can be small comparison between the two. Miss Hempel, for instance, would never have started anywhere with the intention of singing and not have sung after she got there.

Caruso once sang in Buda-Pesth, where he did not please. With another tenor it would have been called a fiasco. "Why don't you go back and try again?" Miss Hempel would say to him. His emphatic "No" was always a mystery to her. That would not have been her way of doing things, as she proved when she reached New York. Berlin had adored Hempel as Baden-Baden had adored Bianchi. In 1909 she arrived here after a year of illness from which she was not yet recovered. Short of her best, and the critics not having knowledge of that best to judge by, small allowance was made for her. "Wait," she said patiently, "when I come back well in the fall it will be different." And it was.

But even in the days that things did not go so happily, she said to me, "I love America, and I *do* want to come back." She did come back, to remain many seasons at the Metropolitan, eventually becoming an American on her marriage with Mr. William B. Kahn, an able, cultured man, who had fallen in love with her when she made her first

FRIEDA HEMPEL

stage entrance on the night of her New York début. An ideal husband he makes, too, with clear business insight of immense value to her career.

The Hempel family was poor, and, as usual in such circumstances, the children were many, twelve in all. It was determined that Frieda should become a concert pianist, having, as each of her eleven small brothers and sisters, a career parentally chosen.

Always she sang, sang all day until her mother's callers were literally driven from the house by it. Meanwhile, she saved up her pennies at a time when their accumulation was difficult, and went to hear great singers from the summits of top galleries. Going home, she would disarrange the furniture to make a stage setting and act out fragments of arias that she had learned by ear.

In spite of all these signs and omens, Miss Frieda Hempel's singing romance did not begin until after she had appeared in concert in her sixteenth year as a pianist. Of the day when Leipsic authorities decided she must become a prima donna, she told me that she felt both glad and sad; glad of the bigger chance promised in singing, but sad to have to start again from the beginning to learn a new calling.

There may have been future prima donnas who worked harder than did Miss Hempel in her girlhood of study in Berlin, but I have not heard of them. One item of it was to repeat three notes of a scale one hundred consecutive times, listening with concentration to each tone. The following day she would take the three next steps of that scale and go through the same process.

Mozart she studied with almost as much minute application, being kept on his arias month in and month out by her teacher, Madame Nikolas-Kempner. To-day there are few who can sing Mozart as does Frieda Hempel. Beyond mere command of technical mastery, the calm beauty, the aristocratic grace of his melodies seem to appeal to her nature, and there is in her that touch of sadness, contemplative rather than real, which responds sensitively to them.

Always she has been shielded. Cramped in means, her parents made the venture of bringing all twelve children from Leipsic to Berlin that Frieda might live at home while she studied. When, after three years of application, the time for her début came, she went about seeking an engagement of the Berlin managers, "In my poor little clothes," as she expressed it, one of her big brothers always accompanying her. Since those days she has sung mainly in gowns from the Rue de la Paix, and not infrequently before kings. So much for the singing romance of a poor girl with a voice, who, incidentally, had learned how to use it.

Perhaps recollection of her less prosperous days

lingered. Arriving the day before her concert at Elmira, New York, Miss Hempel went for a long walk with her maid. Reaching the quiet of the open country, they met a woman with three little children. The trio were threadbare. Getting into conversation with the mother, Miss Hempel joined her, and went with the party as far as their door.

The next day the singer remained in bed resting up for her concert, but no real rest came. She kept thinking of that mother whose dignity had kept her from saying a word about poverty. Then Miss Hempel sent her maid shopping for four outfits. In the evening, before she would sing, she insisted on delivering the things herself. If those children had never before believed in fairies, they must have come near to it when Miss Hempel in concert dress, her diamonds and gold slippers glittering, stepped from a taxi in front of their home.

Impulsive desire of somewhat the same kind once seized Madame Nordica, and as completely. The gardener's children at a place which she had taken for the summer appeared to her as in need of new clothing. In great haste she went shopping for it. I was along. Returning, and to arrange a surprise for the mother, she called out the children and dressed them herself behind sheltering bushes on the lawn, putting the new clothes over their old ones. It may have been due to the hurried dressing, it may have been owing to mistake in sizes, but the littler ones wore trains, and their elder sisters looked like ballet dancers.

Following her début, the limelight began very quickly to play on Miss Hempel. Two years after leaving home to make her first appearance at the Schwerin Theatre as *Queen of Night* in Mozart's *Magic Flute*, the sole rôle she knew, she was called to the Berlin Royal Opera as prima donna. It came about through the Kaiser. The All Highest, having gotten wind of her voice, commanded her to sing in a court concert at the Berlin Castle. Her number was Arditi's *Il Bacio*. It happened to be the Kaiser's favorite selection. As a result, the Grand Duke of Mecklenburg-Schwerin was asked to release her for the Royal Opera. And a request from the Kaiser left no course but compliance.

During the time that she sang in Schwerin, Miss Hempel learned much. Its theatre was noted as a training school for both actors and singers. They gave everything there from operetta upward, and Miss Hempel sang along with the rest, getting both a versatile repertory and stage experience. All told, when she came to this country, she had seventy-five rôles in her repertory, many of them learned and tried out at Schwerin. They loved her there, letting her go loathfully, and in the two years of her stay the Grand Duke had bestowed on her a sample of each kind in his entire stock of decorations.

It happened that she made her Berlin début as *Marguerite de Valois* in a spectacular presentation of *Huguenots* that the Kaiser himself directed. At one of the later rehearsals, with the house in utter darkness except for the stage, where all thought things were going nicely, a voice yelled from the black auditorium, "That man has put his lantern by a barrel of powder! If the scene had been real it would have blown up. What kind of a place is this?" The voice was that of the All Highest.

Not as a matter of consequence, but as one giving curious insight, the Kaiser's favorite opera above all others was not *Fidelio*, nor yet *Tristan und Isolde*, but Donizetti's *Daughter of the Regiment*. He doted on it, a French plot set to music by an Italian.

Rosa Sucher, the once famous dramatic soprano, gave me her estimate one day of the Kaiser. She was knitting at the moment, and her needles clicked angrily as she announced it. Knowing his habit of meddling, which I did not suspect as having ruffled her feathers too, I said, "The Kaiser seems interested in music." The tone in which I spoke must have aroused confidence, for she sharply exclaimed, "He is too much interested in everything, to be much interested 'n anything."

I have heard foreign newspaper correspondents in

Berlin dismiss him with one word, "Superficial," but it seemed to me that Frau Sucher somehow in her estimate covered the ground more completely. Nevertheless, in those days, she was the only one of his subjects from whom I heard such plain speaking.

In the seasons that followed Miss Hempel's Berlin début, she sang in the south of France; at the Paris Opéra with marked success, as *Ophelia* in Thomas' *Hamlet*, and frequently at the Theatre de la Monnaie at Brussels, a city in which she was a great favorite. Once at Ostend, where artists used to delight in singing with the orchestra in summertime and before as cosmopolitan audiences as could be found, old King Leopold of Belgium invited her to sing to him privately at Laaken. Only four people were present, the King, Baroness Vaughn, with whom he was having a violent love episode, Miss Hempel, and her accompanist.

Following this very private recital, the party had *déjeuner*, the King himself serving them. Leopold, whose eagle eye for pretty girls is rather historical, was so taken with the young singer that the Baroness grew furious. I can fancy the demure air with which Miss Hempel carried herself—she can be very demure and still see everything. Also I can fancy the quarter of an hour that the Baroness gave the aged King after the prima donna drove away. But it did not prevent him from sending an equerry next day to Miss Hempel with the decoration of the order of Leopold II, King of the Belgians.

In San Sebastian Miss Hempel sang also in summer-time, with the King of Spain among her auditors, and when he was there in residence. During the season, and almost every season, she sang throughout Germany, in Austria, and in Hungary. When Miss Hempel had appeared in opera for the first time after the war in these last two countries, I asked her, "How is the opera at Buda-Pesth?" I pictured dismal changes brought by the war and revolutions.

"Just the same as ever," she answered. "All the aristocracy seemed to be there. The price of tickets was raised ten times, and, of course, they have to be economical. But then I don't go to Buda-Pesth every week."

In the midst of Miss Hempel's early successful singing across a large section of Europe, along came Mr. Conried, then managing the Metropolitan. With a zeal apparently greater in searching for talent than in paying it when found, he offered her fifty dollars a week to sing at the Metropolitan.

"I will wait until I am worth more to you," she answered. And sang on where she was.

Frieda Hempel is still a hard worker in music. Seventy concerts a season she sings now throughout this country, and in summer has increased the number by singing in foreign capitals; Stockholm was added to her list by invitation of the King of Sweden; San Sebastian, again, by invitation of the King of Spain.

"People say that I should take a big house and entertain," she said to me. "Will you tell me what time I could find for it?" In her early days at the Metropolitan, Miss Hempel did entertain, but in the quietest of quiet ways at her quiet little apartment in the upper 80's. In one aspect those dinners were unique, though she had nothing to do with them. Some prima donnas have had house-wifely talent ascribed them. Madame Schumann-Heink is the only one whom I would trust not to poison me with culinary experiments. In her case the cooking talent is inborn. In Miss Hempel's case it is Rosa. I have never gotten as far as her last name, which should be added on a monument to her genius. She would not only cook those dinners deliciously, but serve them, while all Miss Hempel had to do, and did, was to walk in and sit down at table in a Paris confection looking like a queen in the rather small domain of a New York apartment.

In delightful quarters overlooking Central Park, and where she lived for a number of years, there was a dinner one night that proved out of the ordinary in a sense quite apart from Rosa. Five guests had been invited, four men, and Madame Melanie

Kurt, the dramatic soprano. The four men came, Madame Kurt did not. She was ill. Miss Hempel, the one woman there, managed to guide conversation so skillfully, and two of the men had been born argumentative, that the dinner passed off like a scene from light opera.

Once Miss Hempel fell ill and was supposed to have the influenza. An important concert appearance was at hand. Whether to cancel it or risk the chance of her recovery in time to sing was the racking question. Anxiously hovered over, the patient grew better, then well. Thankfulness reigned. But it reigned briefly. The exact kind of slippers that Miss Hempel wanted could not be found. Without that exact kind of slippers, she refused to sing. She got them. Such little situations are not always due to the artistic temperament; the most of us have had parallel experiences. After a host of real worries, a little one may prove the back-breaking straw.

It is not the unexpected or the willful that distinguishes Frieda Hempel, but earnestness and an endearing gentleness. She and her lovely voice have had a charming singing romance together, and one of the most deservedly brilliant of our times. She is a woman of very big courage; she is very loyal to her ideas of right. Two traits that go to make the best type of American citizen.

CHAPTER X

PASQUALE AMATO

PASQUALE AMATO'S singing romance has carried him far; throughout Italy, to Germany, Paris, London, Brazil, the Argentine, Chile, and finally to the United States, where both the man and his noble voice have been loved well. His adaptability made him one with us, and he speaks our language with a command of its vocabulary possessed by few Americans. That same trait of adaptability has endeared him to the fisher folk of Cesenatico on the Adriatic, where he makes his home between opera seasons.

Cesenatico is a charming corner of the Old World, its villa colony beginning where the village ends, and running its full length of flower-filled gardens along a splendid beach. The three thousand villagers get their living out of the blue waters creeping at high tide almost to the roadway. Their boats' sails, red, orange, and yellow-white, make part of a panorama viewed from the loggia of Amato's villa.

To those simple people, the great baritone is at once a grand personage and a comrade. Basket on

PASQUALE AMATO

arm, he goes marketing among them in the *piazza*,
stopping to chat before one stall and another,
for he is a confidante as well as customer.

Going with him at such times I have delighted in
the scene, full of life, animated, gesticulating over
nothing at all; the piles of fish, mottled silver and
gold, glistening in sunshine; the array of vegetables
placed in elaborate color scheme, as if some artist
were presently to put them into his picture.

Nearby lay the canal, empty from dawn to dark,
when the fishing fleet reached home, furled its sails
and bobbed all night listlessly. In a misty dawn,
at first rose pink, then golden as the rising sun suf-
fused it, the boats would set out again for the day's
catch.

When Italy entered the War, submarines and
mines made fishing in the Adriatic impossible, and
bad days fell on Cesenatico. Remembering their
friend Amato, singing at the Metropolitan, where,
by local computation, he made a new fortune nightly,
each wrote in turn for help. In despair through
trying to respond singly to three thousand wants, he
sent a fund to the village mayor for distribution.
To make that fund larger, his own family menu in
New York became, meanwhile, very simple.

In those delightful days that I spent at Amato's
villa, war was far from mind. But even peace times
held their terrors. The afternoon that I arrived, the

cook departed. Another, who had faithfully promised to come, wired that she had changed her plans.
Both villa and annex were crowded with relatives
and friends; Madame Amato was ill. Dismayed
at the dismal prospect, Amato fainted. The first
I knew of it was when the famous *buffo* Pini-Corsi
came running distraught and shirt-sleeved on the
scene.

Madame Amato, whose chief thought is for her
husband's welfare, appeared at that climax to have
done some thinking. Rising from bed, she ordered
the motor car. Presently, accompanied by her
father and her elder boy, Spartaco, she set out across
the mountains for Florence and a cook. She would
return next day, she told us. A look in her eye gave
full assurance that a cook would return with her.
Meanwhile, three automobile loads of us travelled
to feast at the village inn.

The hour set for Madame Amato's home-coming
with her party struck and passed; two lagging hours
followed it, and still they had not come. Filled
with presentiment of accident, Amato white from
anxiety divided his time between the telephone, trying to get trace of them, and dashing on his bicycle
along the highway by which they would travel.
The day was Sunday, the hardest one in the whole
week to bear suspense. We were all on tension.

In the midst of it, the cook who had changed her mind, apparently rechanging it, appeared.

At last a great cloud of dust rose in the distance, heralding Madame Amato's approach. With a grand flourish the speeding chauffeur brought the journey to conclusion, Amato on the running board and crying rapturously, "The cook has come!"

"*I* have the cook," announced Madame Amato with fine dignity as she alighted. And she had, for never did I see the other cook again.

It has been my privilege to view Amato on the stage in his greatest rôles; away from it, it was my privilege at the villa to view him in still another. At early breakfast, his father and mother at his right hand and the rest of us ranging down the long board, he would cut bread from a huge loaf and pour coffee for each one in turn, only beginning his own meal after all had been served.

To wander casually through Italy is to carry away ineffaceable memories of its beauty; to live in an Italian home is to find in the ties binding lives together there something still more beautiful. About it is an air almost patriarchal and there is about it, too, an air of perpetual youth. The Italians marry young and they live long. Amato, himself, married at Trieste when he was twenty-three. His father's comment had been, "I now have two children where I had only one." The father, it happened, had married at the same age; at fifty-two he had long been a grandfather. Young lives had so overlapped his own that there was no gulf of years making the one generation unapproachable to the other.

Pasquale Amato has two brothers, the one a priest, the other an officer in the Italian army. The priest, visiting at the villa during my stay there, has a lovely tenor voice and serves as soloist at the Naples Cathedral. Tall, supple, handsome, he would likely have proved himself the peer of Pasquale as successful opera singer, had he not chosen the quieter path in which he seems so completely happy.

A concert and ball took place at Cesenatico that summer, and to it Amato's guests were bidden. The festivity was held in a theatre of proportions that would grace a city, and where in winter-time the fisher folk played comedy and tragedy for their own entertainment.

When we arrived, a committee escorted Mr. Amato to the proscenium-box set aside for us, and there, with Italian thoughtfulness, was placed a bouquet for each woman and flowers for the men's coat lapels. The rest of us went home at one o'clock, but Amato remained until dawn with his village neighbors. That is one beautiful trait of Italian life, there is always time for the home, always time for friends. The readiness of custom made Amato just as gladly linger with those simple friends of his, as if no operatic life with its self-centered horizon existed.

And only once, aside from the fainting incident, did anything temperamental thrust itself upon Amato's home tranquillity. One day during *déjeuner*, an organ grinder started up outside. He played through an *Ave Maria* from some now forgotten opera. Then he flung himself abruptly into our midst to take up a collection. Enraged at this behavior, Amato ordered him to leave. He did, but before that there were many, many, words. Safely outside, he started in to play again that same *Ave Maria*. He played it for one solid hour. To have bribed him to go would have meant his return next day. You can picture the scene that he aroused.

Pini-Corsi had his little villa nearby Amato's; Pini-Corsi whom we remember as so gaily humorous at the Metropolitan in *Don Pasquale* and in *Barber of Seville*. That villa of his might, architecturally, have itself lived in a comic opera. On the second story hung a tiny balcony. There Pini-Corsi chose every day to shave himself in public, stopping now and then, his face masked in lather, to have friendly chat with a passing operatic colleague, whose presence his mirror had reflected.

Painters, actors, and some opera singers made up the villa colony at Cesenatico. These last sang to us scenes from *Otello* or, perhaps, *Trovatore* in bathing

costume on the beach, the Adriatic swishing an accompaniment. We also had other things to view
there, at least I had one Sunday morning.

My good friend Giuseppe Campanari, whom we
recall with affection for his singing at the Metropolitan, was not fond of sight-seeing. When his
colleagues on tour started out to view the sights in
a strange city, he stayed at home, asking merely,
"Bring me some photographs of what you see and
then I shall know all about it." But even living in
such seclusion, Campanari appeared to see much.
Indeed he told me of the following little custom
at Cesenatico long before I viewed it.

That Sunday morning, finding none in sight at
the villa, I had sallied out alone. On the beach
ahead of me was an assemblage. At once I knew
the Cesenaticons had come for their weekly dip.
The bath-houses, being private property, were
locked. These good people were, therefore, using
the buildings' shadows as their dressing-rooms, a
shadow to a family. Making quick run for an in-
coming wave, the final garment was dropped on
reaching it. Afterward, this fluttering raiment was
resumed for a pleasant promenade along the sands,
a simple, striped shirt being popular among the
men.

Cesenatico in its seclusion delighted Campanari;
his family and Amato's being close friends they used

in summer-time to go there. But, somehow, Giuseppe found it easier to get into the place than out of it. The train leaving Rimini, the nearest railway station, and joining the main line for Bologna, was generally too late to make connection. Needing money from a bank at Bologna, he made three attempts to reach the town before, at last, he got there. Rushing in a taxi to the bank, he found it closed. "What is this?" he asked excitedly of a passerby.

"*This*," echoed the man, irritated by such crass ignorance, "*this* is the day that comes but once in a hundred years, the centenary of our sublime Cavour."

But Campanari should have grown well seasoned to surprises on his little journeys. He had many. Some of them were, so to speak, self-made. One of this description came on an engagement to sing at the house of Mr. H. McKay Twombly, whose wife, it will be recalled, was born a Vanderbilt. "Where do I and the other singers dine?" asked Campanari of his manager before departing.

"At the Twombly house, of course," was the reply.

Giving proper thanks, Campanari sent this telegram: "Have this evening two tender roast chickens and a bottle of good red wine for dinner." It was directed simply, "The Twombly House."

On arriving the party was met by liveried footman and coachman with an equipage. Somewhat
startled at the sight of such style afforded by a
country inn, Campanari was still more startled on
reaching not the Twombly House but the house of
Mr. Twombly.

His good-natured host, thinking it a freak of the
artistic temperament, continued the joke. When
all were seated at table, a footman brought in a
big silver salver. On it were two tender chickens
and a bottle of good red wine. "Will you have
this?" Mr. Twombly inquired affably, "or will you
take the regular dinner?"

There were many singing experiences, both
strange and picturesque, told in the loggia of
Amato's villa, the stars glowing in a summer night,
the vast stillness broken only by a rush of waters
on the beach or a half-heard song coming from some
villa down the street. Pasquale Amato's share of
these operatic reminiscences was rich.

Very early in his singing life, and following his
début at the Bellini Theatre at Naples as *Germont*
in *Traviata*, Amato sang much at Italy's small opera
houses. And there things happened; fantastic almost
beyond imagination. His entry into operatic life
came quite by accident, for Amato had been destined
for the navy. While preparing for examinations,
he disputed with a professor and knocked him down.

This act, by order of the Minister of War, barred him from state schools. Symbolically speaking, that knock was at the door of art.

Shortly after his début, the young baritone was engaged by Abbé Perosi, director of the Sistine Chapel choir, to sing in his oratorio, *The Awakening of Lazarus.* Almost simultaneously an offer was telegraphed Amato from Lecci to sing *Count de Luna* in *Il Trovatore.* The solos he knew by ear, the ensembles not at all.

Perosi's oratorio presentations ended, the singer rushed to Lombardi, later noted as a singing teacher but then conducting opera. "I have to sing *de Luna* in five days," announced Amato, "and I don't know it." Without wasting time on words, they set to work.

Day and night they kept at it. Two days before the first presentation they travelled to Lecci, Amato studying as he went. Rehearsal took him direct to the theatre on his arrival. Assuming light assurance, he said, "I will sing *Il Balen.*" Which he did, his knees shaking under him for he feared they might ask him to sing more.

His voice put the impresario into transports; he seemed ready to grant anything. Amato, therefore, promptly asked, "Will you kindly excuse me? I am weary." Which was quite true. Personally the impresario escorted his new "star" to the stage door.

Hurrying to his hotel, Amato sought out Lombardi. "I saw nothing but the score; my head was a volcano," the baritone said of the twenty-four hours following.

Lombardi departed to conduct elsewhere, and Amato proceeded to the last rehearsal. Barring panicky moments, all went well. Before the curtain rose the first night, however, new trouble came. The tenor singing *Manrico* had taken offense at the impresario. He left, his only farewell being to the stage hand who carried out his trunk of costumes. To him he had said, "I am making a little journey."

Before the train steamed out of Lecci not only the opera company, but the whole town knew that *Manrico* had decamped. When the impresario somewhat calmed down, he wired for one of the many *Manricos* urged upon him in his agitation. A *Manrico* came. His lofty air promised great things. But to Amato his first words did not, "To-day I will not sing in the rehearsal, I am weary." To sing in his own uncertain state with a *Manrico* who did not know the music promised horrors to Amato. This the public presentation nicely realized.

The new *Manrico* had not a single item of the needed costume. Of course he had never before sung *Trovatore*. This fatal disclosure came at the last moment, when he borrowed everything, from helmet downward, from a chorister.

In the wings, arrogance vanished, *Manrico* stood shivering. During the first trio his helmet, far too big, slipped over one eye and set the audience to tittering. In the second act aggravated fright began to rob him of his voice. Sometimes he sang the right notes, oftener he invented others. Meanwhile, Amato strove mightily to hold his own. The slurs and dots of a score he had so pored over swam before him in the air. Between acts he caught up the notes to refresh his memory, going out to sing exactly as he felt in his boyish heart, that all his future hung on that moment.

In the Convent Scene, as Amato, sword in hand, faced *Manrico*, someone yelled, "Kill him!" This pleasantry started an uproar. When *De Quella Pira* came with its high C, which has saved so many tenors, no high C sounded. In vain Amato in the wings sang that high C instead. But the audience hearing it had also heard *Manrico's* gurgle. With a roar maddened listeners dashed toward the stage to get the tenor. Only a rush curtain saved him.

Amato, wiping the perspiration from his face, sat in his dressing-room. He had risked singing a rôle that he did not know securely, and he had conquered. But never again would he take such chances.

People in viewing an artist singing with absolute poise in any situation would better not call it a heaven-sent gift. Poise, itself, comes, of course, from artistic experience; but the holding of that poise in facing cataclysms is often due to having lived through disturbances aroused by fellow artists.

Just as *Manrico* had given to Amato fine chance to practise concentration, another tenor afforded it at Naples. The opera which celebrated this event was Verdi's *Attila*. The tenor originally cast, instead of decamping, had fallen ill. Another by the name of Brunetti was substituted, after long search disclosed no other. At that time temperament had brought him to the depths as vocal derelict. Only when he felt like it had he sung; at rehearsals his commotions were known to have made impresarios collapse. Tiring of his moods, they abandoned him. That day he was delighted to sing *Foresto* for a fee of four dollars. And a good dinner. The good dinner wrecked his final chance for rehabilitation. As his mood prompted him to eat at once, and before singing, all of Brunetti's arias were gurgled. Appetite well gratified had left no room for voice.

The hubbub that followed during the opera may be best imagined; against it the young Amato, who had set great store by the performance for his career was just beginning, sang from the rise of the first curtain until the fall of the last one. "The so-called artistic temperament!" exclaimed the baritone when he had told the story, "I hold it in horror! Never do I hear the term but I think of the fumes

of stale wine and garlic which Brunetti puffed at me
that day in the ensembles."

After singing throughout southern Italy, Amato
went to Germany as member of an Italian opera
company. In some cities, critics pronounced him
the greatest living baritone. To earn the compliment
he had travelled in third-class cars, trying to snatch
what sleep he could on their hard wooden benches.
Oftentimes he sang twice daily, at an equivalent
of sixty-two dollars a month. Later, in the same
country, he was paid seven hundred and fifty dollars
nightly, and finally signed for eleven hundred dollars an appearance at Berlin, Vienna, and other
centers, a contract which the war unfortunately can-
celled.

During that first German visit, when chance came
for slightly prolonged stay at any point, he and Madame Amato would keep house in a small way. As
his share, Mr. Amato undertook the marketing.
Madame Amato, born in Czecho-Slovakia, had
taught him by rote some rôles in German. To the
language as it was spoken he remained a stranger.
On the twentieth day after arrival he set out to
buy some veal. Very soon he returned without it,
wildly excited. Nor could he explain things; even
his native Italian had grown garbled.

A charming woman and clever, Madame Amato's
stock of oil for calming purposes was, and is still,

inexhaustible. To discover just how bad things were, she donned her hat and went with him to the seat of war. "What is wrong?" she inquired anxiously when they reached the butcher.

"I asked him," retorted that still irate person, "whether he wanted the veal with knuckle or without it. And the oftener I asked him the more excited he got. Then he bawled much, gracious lady. It sounded horrible. But I'll forgive him this time, as I didn't understand it."

To musical artists butchers would seem provocative. Madame Alma Gluck also had an experience with one of them. In summer-time she lives on Fisher's Island. If in need of any other commodity than sand, she sails across to New London to get it. Stopping there at a butcher shop to buy, she found the man both curt and gruff. "Do you know who I am?" she asked indignantly, pausing for full dramatic effect to add majestically, "I am Alma Gluck."

"Well, Alma," he returned serenely, "I never heard of you."

It is the little things in life that aggravate the singing artist. Amato might faint if a cook failed his wife, but on the stage and facing a howling audience he could be relied upon to sing splendidly. Madame Patti could sing on undisturbed after the explosion of a bomb that came near to killing her, but a hissing steam radiator threw her into a nervous frenzy.

Shortly following Amato's début at La Scala, a tragedy came into his life; his voice left him in the midst of a performance. During bitter days that followed, want faced him. Two beings remained steadfast, his devoted wife and Toscanini. And to Toscanini the task of uplifting cheerfulness must have been difficult, for in trouble of a personal kind he would often sit motionless by the hour, his eyes fixed on one spot on the wall.

That early test of want and suffering added to Amato's artistic stature. His voice restored at last, he triumphed on the very stage where it had left him. A South American engagement followed. Beginning with a fee of thirty-three hundred francs a month, in his fifth and final season there he received seven thousand five hundred francs nightly. From South America he came to the Metropolitan.

Amato's splendid singing romance has left his heart undisturbed. Not long ago he said to me: "I have been away from my father and mother for twenty-five years. When my singing days are over, it will mean happiness to me to live out the remaining years with them in Naples."

CHAPTER XI

AMELITA GALLI-CURCI

THE musical romance of Madame Amelita Galli-Curci has been along lines of its own. No incident in it is more curious than that sight-seeing, and not thought of singing, brought her to the United States. She came by a circuitous route, South America, Central America, Havana, finally reaching New York. Three thousand dollars she had left of her earnings from singing along the way; it was her desire to spend it in viewing a country of which she had heard much, and then set sail for Italy. She has not sailed there since.

Alone the extremes that have marked Galli-Curci's career make it remarkable. In girlhood she tramped the streets of Milan to earn her way by giving piano lessons; too poor to pay a teacher, she taught herself to sing; by her unaided efforts she secured a début, and following it appearances at the Constanzi Theatre, Rome's foremost opera house; in Egypt she had sung in opera at sixty-two dollars a night, and in Italy in her beginnings for six dollars a performance. To-day the receipts of a

With the best of good wishes to my friend Mr. Arnthorsa

Amelita Galli-Curci

1921

George W. Besson

AMELITA GALLI-CURCI

single Galli-Curci concert have reached eighteen
thousand dollars; the first six months after her
American début nearly half a million dollars' worth
of her records were sold; her engagements each season average one hundred, one-third in opera, the
balance in concert.   If she had not gained a remarkable triumph, these facts would not have existed.
Therefore, I give them.   Hard facts may make glowing romance.

Amelita Galli, as she was then, made her début
at Trani, a little town in the far south of Italy.
The *Caro Nome* from *Rigoletto* she had sung a short
time before at a musicale in her native town, Milan.
A man who heard her, came up to say that a friend
of his, an impresario, was looking for a good but
inexpensive *Gilda* to sing in *Rigoletto*.   The next
day Signorina Galli sang to him and was engaged.
For the ten performances her total fee was sixty
dollars.

On her first night of opera at Trani, after she
had given *Caro Nome*, an aria that seems always
to have brought her good fortune, the audience went
frantic.   Of the incident she told me, "When I
took the recalls, I could have danced for joy instead
of bowing."   Going with her mother from Trani
to Rome, she called at the Constanzi Theatre, asking
its impresario timidly, "Will you please spare a few
minutes to hear me sing?"   He did; he also engaged

her. When she appeared as *Gilda*, Rome confirmed the verdict of little Trani.

Alexandria, Egypt, came next in the line of engagements, and with an opera company far from the best. Arriving at an unfortunate moment, it went to smash. Cairo had, meanwhile, heard of Amelita Galli, and secured her at sixty-two dollars a night to sing *Lucia*, *Gilda*, *Rosina* and the old repertory. "It paid my way back to Italy, and it gave me a chance to try out my operas," she said smilingly in recalling it.

Getting home on the fare earned at Cairo, Amelita Galli sang throughout Italy as "guest" in opera. At the end of it she made her first voyage to South America, appearing at the Colisseo Theatre, Buenos Aires. All told she has been there three times, once with a company assembled by Mugnone, Italy's famous conductor, and at the Colon Theatre, where she was *Lucia* to Enrico Caruso's *Edgardo*. Other South American engagements that she has fulfilled were at Santiago and Valparaiso, Chile; Montevideo, Uruguay, and in Brazil, where she made a tour with her own company. That tour sent her to wandering northward toward this country.

After each of the first two South American seasons, Madame Galli-Curci had sung at the Teatro Reale, Madrid. There they accepted her as a second Patti; which was gratifying, for the caprice of its audiences has made more than one noted prima donna glad to go home after a single appearance when her contract called for fifteen. It was not so much the mere disapproval of those audiences that the poor things minded, but the terrible babel they made in expressing it. Madame Galli-Curci had no such experiences, ranking as approved coloratura almost with a hero Toreador. But she had another experience, one which, as far as I know, has no counterpart. She sang *Rosina* in the *Barber* in a wheeled-chair. Also the house was packed, and delight uproarious.

Early in that Madrid season, Madame Galli-Curci fell ill of typhus, and lay ill for six weeks. With her enforced absence from the opera, business at the Reale fell ill too. Eight days after the fever left her, and still too weak to walk, the manager came begging that she sing at once. "How can I?" she asked, "when I am not able to stand." His inventive mind promptly suggested *Rosina* in a wheeled-chair.

"We were both broke. He needed the money, and so did I. So I sang," she stated quite frankly, for always in a story of life or in life itself Madame Galli-Curci can be relied upon to say things plainly.

The prima donna's next journey was to prove the first lap in her wanderings toward the United States, for her way was devious. Stopping at the Canary

Islands she rested to regain her strength, presently giving two concerts "to the dearest little people in the world," as she termed them. Of the hardship of twice in succession singing to earn when strength was frail, Madame Galli-Curci said nothing. Regarding this second instance her sole remark was, "They paid two *pesetas a ticket.*"

That season at Buenos Ayres, when she presently got there, brought the singer a welcome which resulted in her heading an opera company of her own to visit Brazil. Principals and chorus were recruited from the forces with which she had been singing. Mocchi, the impresario, lent her scenery and his own private secretary, Bonacchi, as manager. The Brazilian season lasted six weeks; in the first four of it her net profits were one hundred thousand francs.

Then it was that Madame Galli-Curci started northward by way of Central America, giving concerts as she went in Costa Rica, San Salvador, Guatemala, and crossing direct to Havana to sing there with the Bracale Opera Company. At the end of all this, the one hundred thousand francs and more besides appear to have vanished, for when Madame Galli-Curci decided that the one thing in life was to go sight-seeing in the United States, she had only three thousand dollars left. Having heard much of the country she wanted to see two thousand five-hundred dollars' worth, and with the remaining five hundred buy return tickets to Italy.

The prima donna landed in New York in September, a month when opera is dead and those who govern it are resting or busied elsewhere. She knew no one, that is she fancied so, until in Broadway by chance she met a friend of hers and also of Campanini, then directing the Chicago Opera. "You must sing there!" exclaimed this mutual friend. And she did, but not until after he had very nearly pestered the life out of Campanini. Two appearances were reluctantly granted, at five hundred dollars apiece.

It was still the month of September when Madame Galli-Curci left to continue her sight-seeing tour as far as Chicago; there she waited for the opera to open, which it did in mid-November. Meanwhile, she lived on the three thousand dollars which was very soon not three thousand dollars at all.

There is quite another version of Madame Galli-Curci's beginnings here and one fairly established, that she knocked at the doors of the Metropolitan and knocked vainly. In reality, the very first time that Mr. Gatti-Casazza heard the voice of Madame Galli-Curci was in a benefit concert at the Metropolitan on October 12, 1919; the first time that he heard her in opera was at the Metropolitan as

Violetta in *Traviata* on November 14, 1921, when she opened the season under his management.

But one phase of the situation is not affected by this fact. Following her American début at the Chicago Opera, November 18, 1917, almost four years to a day before she sang in opera at the Metropolitan, Madame Galli-Curci had made a reputation so far-reaching that she was chosen to succeed Caruso, who for eighteen consecutive seasons had been the chief figure there on opening nights.

Connected with the Chicago début, at a matinée on her birthday, is an incident that should be mentioned. Campanini came to her dressing-room after the final rehearsal and gave her a four years' contract. He knew in advance what the verdict would be on the part of the public. After her first two appearances, houses were sold out whenever her name was announced; this has been the case ever since.

To his credit, Campanini, realizing that the first contract he had given was unfair to her, changed it at the end of the season, and of his own accord made a new one satisfactory to both. After her phenomenal début, she received among others an offer of thirty thousand dollars to tour the country in opera for the balance of that season, and refused it. The sum in those days looked big to her, but she chose to keep the contract already made and for much less.

Madame Galli-Curci still, apparently, remains staunchly loyal to Chicago; she does not seem one who will ever forget that her first tremendous American success was made there. To Miss Garden, as Artistic Director of the Chicago Opera, she said quite frankly on deciding to sing at the Metropolitan, "I love Chicago and I love to sing there, but in opera in New York I shall sing only at the Metropolitan, exactly as in Chicago I shall sing in opera only with the Chicago Company." Being able to dictate her own terms, which seemed just enough, hers was an unusual position as "star" in two opera companies in the same season.

The singer's repertory is fifteen rôles, four of these she has learned during her stay here, in Gounod's *Romeo and Juliet*, Délibes' *Lakme*, and Puccini's *La Bohême* and *Madame Butterfly*. The *Marguerite* in *Faust* she is anxious to do. I have never heard her, however, express ambition to attempt any part unfitted to her voice.

Her plan of study, evolved in her days of self-teaching, she still follows. Taking the score of an opera to bed with her, she studies it silently until well toward morning. By that time the music of one entire act is memorized. If, however, on reviewing it the next night any point seems insecure, she restudies it. Then it is fixed in her mind. Only afterward does she go to the piano and put the music into her voice. In studying songs she follows that same plan. Being widely read and of developed literary tastes, she never learns any song whose words are not of worth.

Once in so often there comes a singer whom the great public takes unquestioningly to its heart. The situation is identical with that aroused by certain old melodies, loved afresh by each generation on a first hearing. In the case of both singer and melodies, they appear to be ideals that people have long held subconsciously, and that when heard are instantly recognized as the something for which they have waited.

Success in singing is a strange thing; none has analyzed exactly what makes it. Many with seemingly all of the attributes fall short of genuine acceptance. Other singers who utterly satisfy the critical remain without what is termed "drawing power." Jean de Reszke with reams written about his superlative art, and he possessed it, alone never drew a full house. Always the greatest prima donnas were put in the cast with him.

When, years ago, by a series of operatic misfortunes, Nordica, Melba and Eames were missing from Mr. Grau's season in Chicago, Jean and Edouard de Reszke together failed to draw more than a corporal's guard. On alternate nights Calvé would sing to good houses, remaining in bed on the day between to rest up for her next appearance. And Calvé, adored by the public, was far from being as adored by the critical as was Jean de Reszke.

Madame Galli-Curci made her début in that same Chicago, unknown, unheralded. In the first act of *Rigoletto* people frantically welcomed her, and they have gone on frantically welcoming her wherever she has sung in this country. She sprang into favor like the melody that is universally beloved. Behind her lovely voice, there are fine human qualities. What are those qualities? What manner of woman is Galli-Curci herself?

A most astonishing and unusual trait of hers is absolute lack of egotism; it amounts to humility. Here is a proof of it. On June 2, 1920, Madame Galli-Curci wrote to me from the Fort Garry Hotel, Winnipeg, Canada. In the letter she said:

I send you two criticisms written by a very clever critic of San Fransisco. He is a composer himself and will write for me a good song. I told him it *must be good*, and I am sure it will be. I know you will be interested in his clever criticism, so I send it to you. I like the little respectful line for our, (American), old songs.

I turned to those notices by the critic whom Madame Galli-Curci in her letter had twice termed clever. Among the paragraphs that my eye lighted on were these: "The first part of the program was not the distinct success that it might have been had the diva chosen her numbers, and particularly the encores, with more care;" and again, "Some of the runs were not as clearly executed by the soprano and her flutist as they might have been;" and yet again, this time about her singing of a Liszt song, "The singer's face was too placid. Of course we don't want a lot of silly face-making, but when a climax is reached and the singer's expression is almost immobile, the intensity of the thing is not brought out."

Most prima donnas would have put those little digs in a waste-paper basket and not in a letter, and would have said things while doing it. Madame Galli-Curci, ignoring achievements which to many would have brought complete self-satisfaction, had a mind broad enough to still consider suggestions. And she was going to sing his song, which she felt sure would be a good one. Let us hope that it was.

Since landing here, Madame Galli-Curci has sung in her concerts many American songs, not by well-known, but by hitherto unknown composers, and from manuscript. As she explained it, "I wanted to show my gratitude for the kind reception the Americans gave me." The thought behind it was to help along the art of the country. To do it, she sacrificed a place in her programs otherwise given to vocal fire-works assuring far more applause.

To young Americans bringing her good songs she says: "I will sing them." Her interest is genuine. One night at her hotel a lot of American songs had come in; she sang eight of them and wanted to sing more until I reminded her of a concert ahead the next day, and the cold that had caused her to cancel her Hippodrome date the night before.

Her accompanist that evening, and as interested as she, was Homer Samuels, of Minnesota, now her husband, a fine fellow and clever composer whose songs she has so often sung in her concerts. Welsh by descent, the musical gift is with Mr. Samuels a logical inheritance. He studied piano under Lhevinne, in Berlin, at the same time pursuing his studies in composition.

The ideal associations of Madame Galli-Curci and himself are founded on congeniality of tastes, his musicianship doubtless proving of strong value to her, both as accompanist and in the study of new rôles. Taking out citizenship papers early in her stay here, she became on this marriage doubly an American.

Somehow in these days of Amazons, Madame Galli-Curci looks like a portrait painted in the early sixties; hers is the old-fashioned type of refined femininity. Yet she seems able to conduct either a law suit or a contract to successful conclusion, and likely neither judge nor impresario would find that she had omitted any points important to herself.

A good deal of her clever insight comes, perhaps, from much reading, the balance from a caution that marks the Italian. At a German school in Milan, where she studied from her seventh to her thirteenth year, she learned German, French, and English, extensively reading the literature of each in the original. In reading it has been the same with her in Italian and Spanish, the tongue of her mother. She reads much to-day, chiefly poetry, poetic prose, and books on vital topics.

There had been before her one prima donna in the Galli family, the singer's grandmother, Signora Galli-Rota. At upwards of seventy she could still sing to the piano accompaniment of her husband, an opera conductor, then marching toward eighty. Signora Galli was always opposed, though, to her daughter's entering opera; opposed throughout the three years when she toiled alone to fit herself for it, and only reconciled when she heard the frenzied applause given the girl on her début at Trani. It was originally intended that Amelita Galli should be a concert pianist; in childhood her own ambition had been to become a ballet dancer.

In mentioning things to me, she has told of only one bit of encouragement that she had prior to

her début. At Christmas time there was always a
family reunion at the Galli home. Of course, grandmother came and also, of course, she sang the *Una
Voce* or some other such souvenir of her heyday, for
she, too, had been a coloratura.

After the charming custom in Italian house-
holds, where each one at reunions does his or her
share, Amelita gave a little song. At the end of it,
grandmother embraced her, exclaiming, "You will
some day be a greater prima donna than I!" Being
then only five or six years old the import of it went
over her head; the words, though, she remembered.

Gaining her higher education at the Lyceo Ales-
sandro Mazzoni, meanwhile, docilely studying at the
Milan conservatory to become, as destined, a concert
pianist, she had graduated there with honors and
made some appearances in that calling, when, as she
once described it to me, "My father's business
burst."

After this accident it was that the future prima
donna found her voice; unfortunately at a moment
when there was no money to pay for lessons. But
from her twelfth to her sixteenth year her father
had taken her regularly to the opera at La Scala,
and there she had heard the great singers; memories
of the way they did things made the only guide she
had in her self-teaching.

Tramping the streets of Milan to give piano lessons; hurrying home between times to study her scales and *vocalises;* relying on memories of those great ones to help her when she got to her arias, that made up the total of life for Amelita Galli during three years.

Study for opera with a teacher is hard enough work. Without one it must have often seemed to her like sailing on alone in a boat, enveloped in mist; sailing onward and onward not knowing whether her course lay landward or seaward. Galli-Curci has earned all the glory that came to her.

And there has been much of glory. She is still young. Her début was made in 1910, when she was yet in her 'teens. Since then her romance has been that of a popular idol. And the brilliancy of it she owes solely to heaven and herself.

CHAPTER XII

MARIA JERITZA

THERE is in Brno, or Brünn as we knew it prior to the Peace Conference, a touch of the mediæval mingling with modernism. A stronghold castle still keeps its century's old watch on a mountain summit rising from bordering plains, though the town's walls, long ago levelled, have given place to a tree-lined promenade.

Before the World War brought Brünn within Czecho-Slovakian boundaries, the terrace of the Deutcshes Haus, on a plateau high above the town, made in summer twilights a fascinating picture. Dining there at tables dotting the stone flagging was Brünn's social world, its women radiantly beautiful and gowned with a charming taste surpassed nowhere on the continent, for there wealth and culture are things of heredity.

In the background, and on broad stairs leading from the casino, was grouped a military orchestra; uniforms were plentiful; all was light, color, life. Dimly, far below, lay the town, the tree-tops of its promenade, the wide new streets, the narrow winding old ones, their outlines one by one emerging in rows of twinkling lamps. Encircling mountains, on one of them the mediæval castle, closed in a scene, growing dimmer as night and rising mists crept on.

The town, with its old-time air of mystery mingling with modern life, made Brünn a fitting birthplace for the type of singing actress that the world finds in Maria Jeritza. She is of the present, yet not of it. Many forces are eloquently expressed in her many moods, and always those moods are conveyed sincerely, no matter how quick the transition or how fleeting the duration. It is as if her charm of personality abundantly embodied other charming personalities reincarnated in her.

To have observed, as I have done, prima donnas at close range, and down the long way from Adelina Patti to to-day, is to vividly appreciate in Maria Jeritza a new, splendid being of rare talent, and one who, without disturbing prized memories of yesterdays, creates in her own right a supreme to-day.

No stretch of fancy is required to conjure up the scene which she aroused that night at Ischl when, as "guest" from the Volk's Oper in Vienna, she sang for the first time before Emperor Franz Josef. The opera was Johann Strauss's *Fledermaus*, beloved of the Viennese to the point that they demanded it in the repertory of their Court Opera. Her in-

MARIA JERITZA

sinuating charm, the glamour of her personality, delighted the monarch who, preserving youth in his old age, loved art whose youth is eternal.

He, too, doubtless remembering vanished idols, and with years allowing far more memories than have I to draw upon, found that day a rare and captivating new one. His words indicated some such line of thought. Turning absorbed attention from the stage, he sent for his Chamberlain. "Where has Maria Jeritza been engaged that I have not heard her?" he asked tartly of this functionary, adding impatiently, "Why must I always see old women at the Court Opera, when there is such a lovely young one with such a lovely voice?"

To accentuate his enthusiasm in her performance, he commanded the closing curtain rung up and the *finale* of the opera repeated. Following that, whenever Maria Jeritza sang at Ischl, when he was there in residence, the Emperor never missed an opera in which she appeared. Meanwhile, the Court Chamberlain had conveyed to her an invitation to make her début at the Court Opera, Vienna.

Before that night at Ischl, much, very much, indeed, had happened in Maria Jeritza's girlhood and of an order that led far afield from any operatic future. At the age of thirteen she was immured by her mother in a convent, and for life. This came about through the illness of her eldest sister who

lay at the point of death.   Their mother, ardently
pious, made a vow that should the child recover,
Maria, her youngest, was to become a nun.   The ill
child was healed.   The mother, impelled by piety,
robbed her own heart to keep the vow.   And Maria,
whose feet had trodden such a little way in life,
obediently accepted.

Small preparation was needed for her journey
to the chosen convent.   Hers was to be a future of
perpetual poverty.   With a few belongings made
into a little bundle tied in a blue kerchief she arrived at the convent gate.   A tearful embrace, a
lingering kiss from her mother, and she entered a
portal which from without she might never see
again.

There were girl pupils at the convent; the novices
were young in years.   At Maria's age companionship went far toward happiness.   So life there, until
novelty somewhat abated, went forward smoothly.
The Madame Jeritza of to-day told me smilingly
of a consoling factor, "I soon found out that the
nun's habit of dark blue, with its coif of white, was
most becoming."

It was in the still of night that a new phase of the
situation, which she had accepted without thought
and through obedience, flashed upon her.   The
novices slept in a dormitory, where long rows of
cots were placed side by side.   All the others slum-

bered as she lay there that night picturing the time
when she should take the veil. Dressed in white,
with a sweeping train, and crowned with myrtle,
she would advance to the altar. As she knelt there,
her father at the one side, her mother at the other,
her hair would be cut close. One long half of its
glory would be given to her father, one half to her
mother. The spun gold of her hair cut short! She
cried out at the thought.

"What is it?" inquired sleepily the little novice
on the next cot.

"My hair—my hair—" sobbed small Maria.

"Grieve not. It will soon be shorn," and her
comfort-giving neighbor slept again.

"Shorn—shorn," Maria kept repeating between
sobs.

Life at the convent had gone on quite placidly,
barring her temperamental moments. She had willingly agreed to come, and in obedience when she
heard her mother's vow; nor did she bother her head
about a world she had forsaken, for of that world
she knew naught. But to have her hair shorn, carried home, and she left there deprived forever of
its golden halo! That should not be.

In the black silence a recollection came of something she had heard, but up to that instant claiming
no special thought, "If a novice is reprimanded three
times by the Mother Superior, she must leave the

convent—forever." When the rising bell rang at
five o'clock, Maria Jeritza arose calmly at its sum-
mons in the dusk of dawn.

At six o'clock on her way to chapel, the girl carried thread and needle with her. When two pious
novices, who had knelt absorbed immediately in
front of her, arose to leave the chapel, they found
their habits tightly sewn together. Maria Jeritza
had done it. A reprimand, the first, came quickly.

There were two meals a day at the convent.
Maria's youthful appetite craved more. Money she
had none, for already a future of voluntary poverty
was upon her. In a neighboring garden hung apples
to be gotten without price by climbing the high
wall between her and them. It was, perhaps, hunger
rather than thought of the second reprimand
that prompted an immediate invasion.

The wall was high, her novice's habit impeding.
But she gained her goal. Perched perilously on a
swaying branch, she was finding much enjoyment
when on the wall's far side a voice asked austerely,
"Where is the novice Maria?" It was the Mother
Superior who had put the question.

"There," answered all the other novices in chorus,
pointing in horror at their marauding colleague in
the tree.

"Return instantly," came the command.

In the convent garden pupils and girl novices

were in a flutter, not unmixed with delight. From her perch Maria calmly eyed them. Then, with a sigh of longing at leaving so many apples still uneaten, she slid down the tree's trunk.

The novices wore sandals, but no stockings. The wall on that side next the neighbor's garden was smoother of surface than had been the way of her arrival. Sandals made climbing difficult. To hasten matters she took them off, pitching them over the high wall into the convent garden. Then, gaining foothold with her ten pink toes, Maria scaled the wall. The second reprimand kept her long in executive session.

The third upheaval in the convent, where she proved so conclusively her lack of vocation for it, came more, it would appear, from temperament than from premeditation. All had gone for some time smoothly in that atmosphere of peace and innocent companionship, until, one Sunday afternoon in the weekly recreation hour, she engaged in dominoes with a fellow novice, the same who had given words of comfort about her hair.

They played long, Maria ardently. The fellow novice provoked her to sudden wrath. Raising the domino box aloft, Maria smashed it on her head. That brought the third, the final, fatal reprimand. With her little belongings made into a bundle tied in a blue kerchief, and accompanied by a working sister as guard against adventures by the way, she was restored to her home and the world that she had left quite willingly.

When consternation at her sudden reappearance had somewhat subsided, Maria's education, this time of a type to fit her for social life, proceeded vigorously. Piano, violin, and 'cello she took up devotedly; the training of her voice came next under Professor Auspitzer of Brünn, a man who knew his art and how to impart it. In 1910, Maria Jeritza made her début in opera at Olmütz, Austria, as *Elsa* in *Lohengrin*. Born in Brünn in 1891, she had at that time not yet reached her nineteenth birthday.

Madame Jeritza is strongly musical, it is a part of her Moravian birthright. Possessed of vivid imagination and of splendid ability in dramatic expression, one could scarcely fancy her as betraying at any period inexperience in opera. She is of the type of artist to whom age, as such, means nothing. A type that in youth displays the experience of age, and in old age itself sustains the power to embody youth.

Carried into favor at Olmütz by her *Elsa*, her *Elisabeth* in *Tannhäuser*, and her *Marguerite*, she was called five months later, and in 1911, to the Vienna Volk's Oper. Following her début there as *Elisabeth*, Maria Jeritza created in succession the prima donna parts in Nougés's *Quo Vadis;* in

Siberia, by Giordano; in *Manon Lescaut*, by Puccini; in two now forgotten works; *Pompeii* and *Frau Holda;* in Kienzl's *Kuh Reigen;* in *Feuersnot*, by Richard Strauss, and the title rôle in that composer's *Ariadne*, given a première at the Court Opera, Stuttgart, and by command of the King of Württemberg. Later, in a revised version of this last work, she again created the name part at the Court Opera, Vienna.

Madame Jeritza is what is known professionally as a quick study. A record that she made in this direction was learning in two days the prima donna rôle in Puccini's *Il Tabarro*, a feat which came after her engagement at the Court Opera. The singer originally cast for it not meeting Puccini's requirements, he begged that Madame Jeritza undertake not only *Il Tabarro*, but his two one-act operas, *Soeur Angelica* and *Gianni Schicchi*, which made the bill. To memorize in forty-eight hours three operas, though of one act each, was not humanly possible. But, accepting *Il Tabarro*, she mastered it in two days, appearing publicly in it on the evening of the second.

The long list of rôles that Madame Jeritza created in presentations at the Court Opera began with her début there in 1912, in the title part of *Aphrodite* by Max Oberleithner. At that time her full release from the Volk's Oper had not been secured;

this followed in 1913, when the forfeit required on cancelling her contract was paid by the Court Opera.

From that time on, in the seven succeeding seasons which preceded Madame Jeritza's début at the Metropolitan, she created many rôles. Following *Aphrodite* came *Spielwerk der Prinzessin*, a quite modern opera by Schrecker; Weingartner's *Cain und Abel; Frau ohne Schatten* by Richard Strauss; *The Girl from the Golden West* by Puccini carried by Jeritza to fine success; *Violanta* by Korngold, in whose difficult work, *Die Tote Stadt*, she triumphed on her début at the Metropolitan; Schilling's *Mona Lisa*, fantastic and modern in its music; *Jenufa* by Janacek, somewhat Russian in style, but the work of a Czech composer, to whom, as to all composers of that nationality, Emperor Franz Josef showed sympathetic favor; Korngold's *Die Tote Stadt;* Puccini's *Il Tabarro*, and the name part in Strauss's revised *Ariadne*. Beyond these she created the prima donna rôle in Oberleithner's *La Vallière* at the German Opera in Brünn, and the same composer's *Der Eiserne Heiland* at the Court Opera in Buda-Pesth.

As further interesting survey of intensive study accomplished by the singer, other operas to be named and in which she made frequent appearances included *Tosca; Cavalleria; Aïda;* the *Manon* of Massenet; *Carmen; Faust; La Juive; Les Hugue-*

nots (the *Valentina*); *Les Contes d'Hoffman*
(*Julietta* and *Antonia*); *Trompeter von Säckingen;*
Lohengrin; Tannhäuser; Walküre (*Sieglinde*);
Meistersinger (*Eva*); *Fliegende Holländer; Heim-
chen am Herd; Euryanthe; Der Freischütz*, and the
two Johann Strauss favorites of the Viennese,
Fledermaus and *Ziegeuner Baron*. The list could
be extended yet further, for in all Madame Jeritza's
repertory numbers fifty rôles. The major part of
this record in its entirety was achieved between the
years of 1911 and 1921.

Madame Jeritza was singing at the Volk's Oper,
and with her star in the ascendant, when she attracted the attention of Baron Berger, Director of
the Court Burg Theatre. Strongly bent on having
her join the forces of that institution, which in Vienna sustains the rank accorded by Paris to its
Théâtre Française, he guaranteed that in one year
she would be the greatest living interpreter of Joan
of Arc.

Reinhardt, the noted producer, was the next to
endeavor to win her from the operatic stage, and
that she might appear in his pantomimes given in the
grand style. Franz Lehar, composer of *The Merry
Widow*, saw in her the ideal prima donna to create
his operetta rôles.

Each man, from his own point of view, had seen
reflected in her versatile performances a different,

individual appeal. She, however, was not to be swerved from the ideal of her life—the opera, for which she had toiled prodigiously.

Pierre Hamp added yet another appreciation to those of Berger, Reinhardt, and Lehar. He saw her with a poet's eyes in his *Les Chercheurs d'Or*, a book in his series, *La Peine des Hommes*. It tells of Vienna during the crash in 1919, when European profiteers, *Searchers for Gold*, scurried to the Kaiserstadt to batten on a want that sacrificed all for bread. A group of these profiteer characters is described by him as viewing at the opera the performance of Maria Jeritza as *Ariadne*, a performance of such moving, humanizing power that even their encysted hearts were softened.

Madame Jeritza can only be portrayed in color; the gold of her hair, the hazel blue of her eyes, with black lashes; the health-tint of her skin. These heighten, but they do not constitute the bigger part of her appeal, which lies in her magnetism, her fascinating personality, and her womanliness.

There is about her no aloofness, no self-absorption. Rather, hers seems the gift of projecting herself into another's feelings, and making them her own. I have seen her give ill-spared hours to testing the voices of young Americans. Her truthfulness was direct and piercing, to save them, when they lacked talent, to help them if they possessed it. But never did she resort to temporizing or subleties that would have made either them or their teachers her friends at the cost of truth.

Madame Jeritza's gestures, her poses, her facial expression convey the meaning of her thoughts as clearly as do her words. In passing from that life away from the stage to life on it, she seems merely to be projecting her own eloquent personality into a new situation, which she sustains with intense sympathy for the characterization.

Life has held another romance for Madame Jeritza aside from her singing one. Her marriage with Baron Leopold Popper de Podhragy united her with a descendant of great musicians. He is a grandson of the famous singing teacher Mathilde Marchesi and the distinguished Salvatore Marchesi, Marquis de Castrone de la Rajata, whose only surviving daughter, Blanche Marchesi, herself a noted singer and teacher, became on her first marriage the wife of Baron Popper de Podhragy. His family was ennobled in 1791 by Emperor Leopold II, brother of Joseph II, and son of Maria Theresa, to whom a banker ancestor of the Poppers not only loaned the money to help prosecute her war against the Prussians and save her throne, but placed at her disposal his entire fortune down to his gold, silver and jewels.

The grandfather of the present Baron Leopold, and owner of great tracts of forest in Austria and Hungary, was the first in the Empire to install steam saw-mills, amassing a large fortune. The young Baron's father in turn continued the business, and the family, one of the richest and most prominent in the old Austro-Hungarian Empire, still possesses vast forests and estates in Eastern Europe.

Baron Leopold is highly educated; following his graduation from several High Schools, he studied in the Universities of Nancy and Vienna, taking in the latter the course in jurisprudence. Afterward, he became connected with the business founded by his ancestor, and has been successful in it. His collection of old art is one of the most important in Austria.

The life of Madame Jeritza at Vienna held both artistic and social charm; in the one aspect of it an idol of the public, in the other a favorite in high circles. Frequently a guest of the archduchesses, whose love of art they shared in common with the Hapsburgs, she was appointed in 1917 by Emperor Karl as Chamber Singer, the last upon whom this title was conferred prior to his dethronement.

The remainder of Madame Jeritza's singing romance bids fair to be lived out in America; the triumph she achieved here brings this as logical conclusion. On her New York début at the Metropolitan, November, 1921, in *Die Tote Stadt*, she aroused a welcome such as is seldom given there; her next rôle, *Tosca*, brought her art's accolade as one of the world's greatest singing actresses.

CHAPTER XIII

PRIMA DONNA ROMANCES I

JEANNE GORDON—ROSA PONSELLE—LUCY GATES

DESCENDED from Scotch, French, and English ancestors, Miss Jeanne Gordon has inherited a combination of national traits; the artistic temperament, the logical mind that so seldom goes with it, and an ability to surmount difficulties before considering them. Born in Canada, where her father was for eighteen years a member of Parliament, she is familar with political life, with the diplomacy necessary to success in it, and has the spice of wordly training which comes from association with bright minds and distinguished people.

In girlhood she often sang to their family friend Sir Wilfred Laurier as a source of inspiration while he was writing his speeches. Her father with a tenor voice beyond the ordinary, and a trained musician, loved best of all music the old Masses of Mozart, Haydn, and Schubert. These the two sang much together. Piano she studied from childhood; her general education was completed at To-

LUCY GATES
Photo by Charlotte Fairchild

JEANNE GORDON   ROSA PONSELLE
Photo by Mishkin   At the time of her début in opera
Photo by Mishkin

ronto, at whose conservatory her voice was schooled. Altogether this gave a fuller background to her life than falls to many young prima donnas. And with no thought of such a future ahead of her.

Married to an American, Lieutenant Ralph Trix, their home was in Detroit. Through patriotism, he left a profitable business there, and entered the United States Navy during the World War. Coming with him to New York to remain that she might see him briefly between cruises, Miss Gordon looked about for something to do; the pay of a naval officer was small, and she wanted to add to it by her own earnings.

Two months after deciding to turn her voice to account, Miss Jeanne Gordon became a "war prima donna." All that followed was but a prelude, and a brief one, to her engagement at the Metropolitan Opera House. There, on the night of her début, Miss Gordon's real singing romance opened.

For her first tour, which was with the Creatore Opera Company, she learned in six weeks the two rôles of *Amneris* in *Aïda* and *Azucena* in *Il Trovatore*. Creatore's tour ended, she returned to New York and signed for another tour with the Scotti Opera Company, learning for it the *Suzuki* in *Madame Butterfly* and *Lola* in *Cavalleria*. Meanwhile, three telegrams came to her from the Metropolitan, each asking for an interview.   All remained unanswered.

"Do you think you are too good to sing here?" asked Mr. Gatti-Casazza, when finally she reached his presence at the Metropolitan Opera House.

"I think I am not good enough," was her disarming answer.   Whether this sprang from youthful modesty or the wisdom of political training, the result was the same.   The real foundation of reluctance, however, was thought of her happy home life in Detroit.

Had not family encouragement strengthened her, it is doubtful whether Miss Gordon would have signed the contract at all.   Lieutenant Trix on hearing of the Creatore engagement entered upon during one of his cruises, had said, "Go ahead."   Her musical father, travelling all the way to New Orleans, heard her as *Azucena* and *Amneris*.   His verdict was, "You have chosen wisely."   This commendation was all the dearer, because only one week later he died.   Miss Gordon, herself, said that without knowledge of that approval she would never have been happy in opera.

Jeanne Gordon had sung the first two engagements in spring and early autumn respectively; that same autumn came her début at the Metropolitan. Several new parts had to be learned before its season opened.   Altogether during her débutante year, she memorized sixteen rôles and studied the action; among these were the *Brangaene* in *Tristan and Isolda*, done in English, *Eboli* in a special revival of Verdi's *Don Carlos*, and parts in *Oberon* and *Boris*. This big undertaking meant hard study; oftentimes the whole night through until four o'clock in the morning, kept awake by drinking strong black coffee.

There were endless rehearsals at the Metropolitan; one came on the day of her début, and lasted for hours. Going home too tired to rest, she returned early to the opera house. Listlessly she dressed as *Azucena* for the first act. To her it seemed but one more of the usual appearances she had made with little companies.

On her way to the wings she met Mr. Egnini, the stage manager, who had served in that capacity with the Scotti company. In frenzied excitement he exclaimed, "Try, try to-night with all your might! If you never do well again, do well now."

This aroused her from apathy to realization. Mr. Egnini had trained her in the action of *Azucena;* mingling with pride as her teacher was the sympathy that all good stage people have for each other. The touch of human emotion had brought her out of her trance of tiredness. This was America's greatest opera house and she was making her début.

Going onto the stage, the sound of the orchestra

below blinding footlights set her aflame. When she passed back through the wings after doing her part in the first act, it was as accepted prima donna at the Metropolitan. Before that there were many curtain calls, several for her alone.

Hurrying to her dressing-room, Miss Gordon took off her *Azucena* wig, beads, and costume, and started to get into street dress. Rushing in to congratulate her, Egnini and some singing colleagues stood aghast at the sight. "What are you doing? Why do you undress?" they asked in chorus.

"To go home," she answered briefly.

"To go home?" they echoed all at once. "Why, you've got two more acts to do!"

Brought back for a second time that night to reality, Jeanne Gordon dressed and sang out the part.

The oldest opera-goers received a thrill on the night of Miss Rosa Ponselle's début at the Metropolitan, but a fact jealously guarded was that there came near to being a failure instead of a triumph. Enrico Caruso saved the situation.

Following the general rehearsal of *Forza del Destino* in which she was to make her appearance, Miss Ponselle caught cold. When her début night came she sat in the "star" dressing-room in tears and with white spots in her inflamed throat. Up to the last moment she had fought, and apparently she stood good chance to lose.

Carmela Ponselle, her elder sister, who had dropped all thought of a career to devote herself solely to the new prima donna, their teacher, William Thorner, and one or two others clustered anxiously about the débutante. Just beyond the closed door was an empty stage cleared for the performance; a crowded house was expectantly waiting. Rosa Ponselle must appear.

It was no new scene for those dressing-room walls to look down upon. They had witnessed many of them. But the risk for a prima donna already famous is one thing, and the risk for a débutante who has still all to prove is quite another, one near to tragedy.

To spur on her courage, Thorner was saying, "Rosa, if you give out only fifty per cent of what you *can* do you will win." Carmela with trembling hands was applying make-up where tears had washed it away. Then Caruso, cast to sing with her, entered. He heard the few words there was time to say, and left, running. "My own remedy," he said on returning, too much out of breath to say more. And set to work. As the minutes flew he kept at his task, carefully, with the skill of practice. "*Now* you will sing," he said. Those who heard Rosa Ponselle that night agreed with him.

Leading up to this climax which for Miss Ponselle ended happily, her path had been rough. Its beginnings had promised little; she had sung in the hubbub and smoke clouds of a cabaret; in moving-picture theatres; in vaudeville. Between the three she had earned her own living from the age of thirteen.

There was something pathetic in the incident with which her singing career started in childhood—going to a moving picture theatre with nothing to sing to its manager in a "try out" but hymns. To be sure he told her brusquely to go home and learn other things with more "pep" in them, and he engaged her at fifteen dollars a week. But before that her young voice in those hymns had made him shed tears.

This contract ended, her cabaret singing in New Haven followed. There Carmela joined her, for Rosa, with larger initiative, had gone on ahead to break the way. In childhood both had sung in the children's choir at a church in Meriden, Connecticut. Into the cabaret they carried with them this atmosphere of childish innocence; slender girls earning their bread in the one way they knew how, with the one gift that had been given them. In the smoke haze they created their dream of a future, not a lofty one, but they held fast to it—to go to New York and sing in vaudeville; of course together, for the two were inseparable.

Of the discovery of Rosa Ponselle's voice sensational stories have gone the rounds, though they were fiction. In reality Carmela was the first to study. Rosa's intention to do the same was discouraged. "One singer in a family is enough," Mr. Thorner had said when she asked him to teach her. The main reason was, it seems, that he did not at all like her method of singing.

Charm of personality secures much when its possessor would have things, and Rosa Ponselle had her own way very soon. In two weeks, her musical gift had brought her so far that her teacher predicted she would be singing at the Metropolitan in six months. In reality her début came even earlier. Meanwhile, she was at the studio from two in the afternoon until nine at night, when they put her out.

Madame Nordica once declared that it took the sacrifice of three lives to make one prima donna's career. Rosa Ponselle's career brought no such triple tragedy. But the fact remains that Carmela, ever faithful, gave up for four years all thought of her own singing life that she might devote every energy to her sister. Not until Rosa's feet were firmly planted in the kingdom of music did Carmela return to her own preparations to journey there.

Miss Ponselle's singing career has not bristled with adventures brought by wandering, but has gone calmly forward; nor with her has there been a toiling upward in opera after she got there. Instead, she has continued steadily in first rôles in a great opera house. To her lot it has fallen to sing with Caruso oftener than has any other young prima donna. In his very last appearance at the Metropolitan she sustained her accustomed companion rôle to his in *La Juive*.

Miss Lucy Gates in her singing career has had no such crown of calm. But each artistic career is so different from the other that fascination lies in the very contrast. Miss Gates was about starting in on that romance of hers when I met her in Berlin. At the Royal Opera they needed just then an Ännchen for *Weber's Der Freischütz;* as *Ännchen* she presently appeared there, without rehearsal. Beyond bowing to the Devil, who was supposed to be invisible, all went well.

Her next singing adventure at that same Royal Opera came shortly afterward as *Titania* in Thomas' *Mignon*. She had twelve days in which to learn the music and action, and the long spoken dialogue in German, a language that she spoke insecurely. One rehearsal was allowed her. To it came the rest of a disgusted cast, every one of whom had been

singing in *Mignon* for full twenty years.   So they
rehearsed it backwards, beginning with the last act.
If she did well as *Titania*, Miss Gates was promised
a two years' engagement.   She did well, and she
got it.

Of the performance Miss Gates told me later,
"Chorus and orchestra I had never heard until that
night when I went on the stage.   As I didn't know
my entrances the stage manager would push me out
at the right one, and some friendly singer would
push me back when I ought to go.   Meanwhile, in
that awful dialogue which the rest rattled off like
so many alarm clocks, I aired my panicky German.
But, when the Polonaise came I planted my feet
on the boards and thought, 'Thank Heaven!   Here
is something I can do all by myself.' "

Having suffered thrills of her own in *Mignon*,
Miss Gates gave some presently to the Berliners
in the presentations of *Huguenots* put on at the
Royal Opera in spectacular style, and under the
Kaiser's personal direction.   She was cast as the
Page and had to enter on horseback.   Before leaving
home in America, Miss Gates had been used to
galloping bareback over the western prairies.   On
the first night of *Huguenots*, starting at the back of
the stage she raced her horse down to the footlights
and reined up suddenly.   The frightened orchestra
players started to flee thinking horse and rider would

land among them. After she left Berlin and went to the Royal Opera in Cassel as coloratura prima donna not a *Fräulein* could be found who would risk the *Page* in *Huguenots* on horseback.

The best chapter of Lucy Gates' singing romance, however, began in her own land after the war broke. I met her then, most unexpectedly, in New York. "I have fifteen dollars in my pocket and the clothes on my back," she said cheerfully. That was all that Lucy Gates had left after five years of toiling and moiling in opera in Germany. Going over to London to arrange details of her contract to sing at the Covent Garden Opera, war was declared as she arrived. Everything she owned, even her stage costumes, reposed at Cassel, for her stay in England was supposed to be a brief one. "But I am here," she ended quite gaily. So were artists of most other countries, and as refugees all seeking engagements where very few offered. But Miss Gates seemed to pick contracts out of the air.

Hers is the gift of action with few words. Soon she appeared in opera with the American Singers, after that she sang in concert. Before three years passed she had sung not once but several times from Toronto to Texas, from New York clear to the Pacific coast and then up and down it. She had sung with the principal orchestras and she had sung in recitals alone.

Miss Gates summed it up lately in a way touching and characteristic, "Do you know what has pleased me most of all? To be able to lift the last mortgage on my mother's home at Salt Lake City." This ability followed her first successful tour as singing impresaria with her own opera company. Hungry for opera at the end of three years of concertizing, and no doors being opened to her, she got together a company herself. Aside from Miss Gates, the sole professionals in it were a *basso* with some opera experience and a light opera tenor whom she had taught. The rest were amateurs recruited at Salt Lake City.

Miss Gates schooled her forces in acting, taught the steps to the ballet; stagemanaged; directed the lighting; collected the scenery; designed some of the costumes and rented others; did the bookings; engaged the special trains by which the large personnel travelled. Her staff consisted of her brother as conductor, who also drilled the chorus, and one publicity man. The repertory was *Traviata*, *Faust*, and *Romeo and Juliet*. In one of these, *Traviata*, she likely set a precedent by singing *Violetta* eight times in six days. Tours were made in the inter-mountain region; for four seasons the undertaking has proved an artistic and financial success. Miss Gates plans to repeat it annually.

Her fearless courage is of the pioneer kind, coming as birthright to Americans born of a stock long in this country. But the technic that helped her in drilling her company was gained at the Royal Opera in Cassel during a three years' stay. The personnel being small and everything sung from *Parsifal* to operetta, she would appear there as coloratura prima donna one night, and the next in a small rôle, or sometimes, three of them in a single performance.

The singing adventures of Miss Gates in her own country have been many, and they have brought her near to the heart of a very large public. Always, too, she seems to have met situations on the level of a sympathetic understanding. Two such incidents were among those she has told me. One night a number of people entered the hall toward the end of her concert. At its close they thanked her for the little they had heard, explaining that two automobiles in which they started had broken down; eventually they arrived in a motor truck. Too tired to stand, Miss Gates sat down on a chair and sang to them most of the songs they had missed.

At another time, after a *Faust* presentation with her own company, a boy came behind the scenes to see her. He had walked twenty miles to get there; that night he would again walk twenty miles back home to a ranch to reach it in time to milk many cows. To Miss Gates he said, "I am richly rewarded." On the surface, this may not seem ro-

mance. But romance of the best sort underlies it.
The singer who can command such incidents may
count herself lucky. They mean that she and her
songs will remain forever endeared as one.

Lucy Gates knows how to sing. In practically
proving it to her public, she resembles strongly her
compatriot Theodore Roosevelt, accepting obstacles
only as something to be overcome. Had she been
born an Indian her title would have been Chief
Unafraid.

CHAPTER XIV

PRIMA DONNA ROMANCES. II

Lucrezia Bori—Marguerite D'Alvarez—Florence Easton

FACING the Piazza del Duomo in Milan is an operatic boarding-house called Pension Bonini. It has two dining-rooms. One with a monumental silver-plated épergne exactly in the middle of its table was for the elect, those who had engagements; the other, without épergne, was for those who some day hoped to have engagements or were merely studying singing. It was in the dining-room without épergne, where all were equals, that I stumbled on the beginning of Miss Lucrezia Bori's singing romance.

Up to that time, full of promise, she had made a single appearance; at the age of five and in her native Spain. The benefit concert in which she sang was for soldiers' orphans; her selection *Il Bacio*. At the end of two pages she made a mistake. Calmly directing the accompanist to begin again at the beginning, she sang it through, that time to her satisfaction.

LUCREZIA BORI
Photo by Mishkin

FLORENCE EASTON
Photo by Mishkin

MARGUERITE D'ALVAREZ

Of the many gathered at table in the Bonini dining-room, Miss Bori was the most attractive figure
and a lovely one, for she had just emerged from girlhood. Her father was with her; a small Spaniard,
very dapper, exquisitely mannered, and a chaperon
whose tact and watchfulness were unequalled by any
dowager whom I have met. At his left sat the radiant daughter, at his right a youthful Italian, an
opera conductor. The byplay was engaging.

The youthful conductor was ardent; the daughter
demure, but given to occasional dazzling smiles in
his direction; the father, whose small figure seemed
to grow in size from the start of a meal to its conclusion, loomed as adamant, and with one object,
to preserve his child's affections intact for the
stage. And father's ear it was that caught and held
most of the glowing strophes designed for another.

Until his death that faithful father travelled with
Miss Bori on her operatic journeys, and one can
imagine the admiring nothings that reached his ear
and got no farther on moonlight nights on ship decks,
and elsewhere. He surely heard it all with a smiling,
flattering attention, just as he listened to the ardent
youth at Pension Bonini, but always between the
speaker and his daughter his small, guardian figure
doubtless rose as a blank wall.

One day father and daughter were missing from
the dining-room without épergne. She had gone for

a "tryout" at Pia and, of course, he with her. But in getting there she lost him. You can picture the young conductor's satisfaction when he heard of it. Miss Bori later told me the near-tragic story, not as it concerned him, but herself and "father."

Seating her safely in a railway compartment, the old gentleman hurried off to send a telegram. As he emerged from the station what should have been his train left it. Without money, without ticket, which in Italy is serious, and without her omnipresent father, Miss Bori went steaming toward Pia. Unaccustomed to being alone, except for sleeping purposes, the young girl was in a panic. The train guard, being an Italian, knew, of course, that they were giving *Pagliacci* at Pia. So when she explained to him that she was *Nedda*, he believed her. With her angelic face and arch ways, he would doubtless have believed her had she told him her name was Lucrezia Borgia instead of Bori. At Pia, when she got there, her charm again prevailed, and she passed the station gate undeterred. Making straight for the opera house, a new dilemma confronted her at the stage door, and one that filled her with terror. From within came a torrent of hisses; the audience had just listened to a tenor of whom it disapproved. With the hisses mingled howls; then came pandemonium. Pia, though small, was particular about its singers.

Shivering at sounds which might the next night be repeated when she sang to them, Miss Bori stood outside, too scared to enter. There the doorkeeper found her and after much persuasion induced her to go with him to the impresario. Already a frantic telephone message from father had reached him. The family reunion, which took place two hours later, was said to have made Pia shed tears. Several years afterward, when motoring through the little town, its inhabitants recognized Miss Bori and cheered her, shouting "Our Nedda."

The real début of Miss Bori was made at the San Carlo in Naples, where the radiant daughter, accompanied always by the fragile father, made a picture appealing to the sentiment of the Neapolitans. Following that engagement Miss Bori returned to Milan, eligible to the Bonini dining-room with épergne, for she was singing at La Scala. In Paris she sang first with the Metropolitan forces during their visit there, and with Caruso in Puccini's *Manon Lescaut*. Puccini, himself, came to Paris for the performance. In speaking of it, he told me that not having heard the opera for eight years, it interested him as a new work. Then he added something of curious interest, "Once I have written an opera it passes from memory, and it scarcely occurs to me to play some fragments from it."

In the years that followed, the tragedy in Lucrezia Bori's life developed a courage and an initiative strongly at variance with Pension Bonini days. When her voice left her, and in the heyday of her success at the Metropolitan, it needed a very brave heart to keep up. Courage never forsook her. If sad things in life are happily ended it is needless to dwell on their harrowing details. One may say, though, that for Lucrezia Bori to live on and on until months made years and to be denied, meanwhile, self-expression in singing, must have meant lying conscious in an open tomb.

Hope never quite flickered out; she still could pray. And with hope in her heart and prayer on her lips she made a pilgrimage, vowing at the end of it to pattern her life after that of St. Francis of Assisi if she were healed. She was healed, as we all know. No more moving welcome could well be given than was hers when she returned with her voice restored to the Metropolian that loved her.

Lucrezia Bori's romance is of voice and soul; her young life has been dual. Reaching success she was thrown out into darkness to emerge restored to art with developed strength to sustain it. There is about her a poise, not untinged with sadness, an absolute self-reliance making strong contrast to the shielded, sheltered girl without initiative whom I saw in Milan, before success, then catastrophe, then success again had molded her through triumph, through hope, and through prayer that was answered.

Far from tragedy, though perhaps not so far, for often her moods and oftener her singing show close acquaintance with it, is Marguerite D'Alvarez. We knew her first at the Manhattan Opera House; following that she sang at the Kingsway Opera House and Covent Garden, London, where during war time and air raids all her concerts were given for charity; Boston has heard her at its opera, and also Chicago, with whose forces she sang in New York.

Dark, luminous eyes; transparent whiteness of skin; masses of dark hair, and the commanding figure of a young Brünnhilde combine to visualize Marguerite D'Alvarez. But hers are other and still greater charms; a mysticism that gives unfathomable depths to her eyes; a temperament that suggests at one moment lilies, at the next fiery jungle blossoms. And her mind is the mind of a poet. She is of Inca descent; perhaps that explains much.

Give such a woman a voice capable of conveying poignantly the life tragedy held in a modern song of four lines or of singing in lilies Schubert's *Litany for All Soul's Day* and you have a figure more fitted to create and live romance than any novel will likely offer.

Of course, such an exotic being as Marguerite

D'Alvarez required an unusual beginning of the singing life. And she got it; at the age of sixteen. Her father was Minister of Foreign Affairs in Peru. The Colombian Ambassador to Great Britain and his wife were respectively godfather and godmother to her in baptism. At a convent she learned some Spanish songs of love, and other things; she also learned some amorous Spanish dances. These were scarcely a part of the good nuns' curriculum, but even to a convent sub-débutantes take each their little grain of worldy knowledge; when all these grains are assembled for communal distribution, they make, perhaps, an educational total larger than one would suspect.

Emancipated by graduation from this gentle atmosphere, Miss D'Alvarez journeyed at the age of sixteen to London, where she visited her godparents at the embassy. During her stay a musicale was given there; the diplomatic circle and many outside it were invited. On the afternoon set for it a dense fog stopped all traffic. The invited guests by starting early before the fog-pall reached its climax managed to get there. Not one of the musical artists, however, except the accompanist, put in an appearance.

The hostess' predicament was trying. Sympathetically, Miss D'Alvarez remembered her Spanish accomplishments. "I'll sing some Spanish love songs for your guests," she proposed, adding hastily, "some I learned at the convent." The amorous dances she left wisely unmentioned.

"A young girl learn Spanish love songs at a convent!" cried the startled godmother. However, the moment was not one for quibbling; there must be a program. Marguerite was allowed to give it. To add a picturesque touch, the pious godmother got out a beruffled silk dress and lace mantilla which she had always worn to Sunday bull-fights. Donning these, the future prima donna made her début.

That afternoon, through her gift of creating pictures with the songs she sings, Miss D'Alvarez lured her hearers to Andalusia and other sections; the London fog had seeped in, dimming the candles and palling all else with its drab mist, but the radiant creature effaced thought of it. By the time her Spanish dances came, dances which the early ripeness of her figure made entrancing, everyone was insisting that some trick had been played them, and that this was a new professional "star."

Soon afterward Marguerite D'Alvarez crossed the channel to study at Brussels; a London fog had started her on her singing way. At Rouen she made her début as *Délila* in Saint-Saëns' *Samson et Délila*. A contract was handed her to sign after the first rehearsal there. Fortunately, it was not an extended one. From Rouen she went to Marseilles to sing in *Favorita*. She pleased enormously, but the tenor appearing that night with her did not, although she, herself, regarded him as fairly good. Presently, the audience broke into a brutal uproar, they would have none of him.

Going down to the footlights Miss D'Alvarez stood with folded arms. A little while before, they had stormily redemanded her *Mio Fernando;* being young and beautiful, she was good to look upon as she stood there staring at them. The noise quieted. "If you accept me," she announced briefly, "you accept him." This they proceeded to do.

From Marseilles, Miss D'Alvarez went to sing in opera at Algiers. There an Arab Chief fell in love with her; sent her a pair of white Arabian horses, and offered himself in marriage. Not relishing the thought of singing *Mon cœur s'ouvre à ta voix* for the rest of her life in the desert, sand storms permitting, horses and chief were left behind when she departed for Milan.

There as *Amneris in Verdi's Aïda,* Miss D'Alvarez sang at La Scala, moving forward absorbed in her profession, and naught besides. Sending one night for a cup of coffee during an *Aïda* performance, a call boy brought it to her, and straight out on the stage. The sight of her as *Amneris* had made him forget that all else existed. There are women who become universally an object of love. It is inconvenient for the object, but unavoidable to all concerned.

Love is the greatest thing in the world, if its object of adoration is not changed too frequently. In this instance which follows, however, love has remained constant. And it is the romance of two opera singers.

Daudet, in his *Les Femmes d'Artistes* took a whole volume to show that no man and woman can build careers side by side and maintain happiness. A multitude less able than Daudet has shared his dismal premises, and a still greater multitude frankly regards one singing partner in life as a calamity.

The day of their marriage Florence Easton and Francis Maclennan promised one another never to separate, no matter how fine the engagement might be that was offered to only one of them. The promise has been kept faithfully. Theirs is a romance with the added glamour of an operatic background.

Though Florence Easton's life started in Yorkshire, England, she was brought so early to Canada by her singing parents that she may be looked upon as a Canadian. Studying first as pianist at the Royal Academy, London, she forsook that career in favor of singing. Still in girlhood, her voice was trained in Paris. Returning to London she sang for a time in concert, then went into opera in one of the two Moody-Manners companies touring Great Britain. Engaged at that moment in the other branch of the Moody-Manners organization was Francis Maclennan, a braw Scotchman, whose mission in life it was to sing a long list of tenor heroes. Neither then knew of the existence of the other. But they soon found it out. When they met, both discovered that they were in the world for no other purpose than loving one another.

Sometimes they sang together. You can fancy what the music meant to them; music written by older hands for just such young hearts and voices as theirs. And you can fancy, too, how they stirred youthful pulses by the tender passion in their singing and brought to the maturer memories of dear yesterdays.

It went on for some time, this romance of the opera, for each had a path in life to tread, and each had but just started in it. Finally a day came when they were singing in London; she was appearing with one company, he with the other in a different part of the city's vastness. But the same London haze that tones the harshest outlines of the old town to things of beauty beloved by painters, rested on both.

At that juncture which had brought them so near together, their romance had gotten as far as fixing a day for the wedding. Here the writer of fiction would have ended. As a chronicler of romantic fact my task is just beginning, for the best part of all is to come. Young love promises much, but it is the practical fulfilling of those promises throughout married years that makes the morning stars sing together. A vocal occupation which they, perhaps, enjoy infrequently.

On their wedding day, Florence Easton's engagement automatically ceased. Her husband's re-engagement in one Moody-Manners Opera Company was jeopardized because he had bereft the other Moody-Manners Opera Company of its most treasured lyric soprano. To be quite material, it may be stated that Mr. Maclennan had that day the British equivalent of seventy-five dollars in his pocket.

However, that very day of all others, Francis Maclennan sang to Mr. Henry Savage, who was gathering forces for his presentations here of *Parsifal*, and was engaged. For Miss Easton, though, there was nothing. Together they came to America where he sang almost nightly; her rôle was silence.

Later, Puccini's *Madame Butterfly* was given an American première by Mr. Savage. Florence Easton sang the heroine, and in the company of which her husband was a member. The next break came when Maclennan accepted a call to the Berlin Royal Opera to sing heroic Wagnerian rôles. By stringent rule of that institution, husband and wife could not both

be given a contract. Now and then Miss Easton
was allowed to sing a *Butterfly* performance.

It takes rather a stretch of imagination to picture the German Kaiser in the rôle of a Good
Fairy. But in his day he did many a kindly deed
with temperamental impetuosity. A prima donna
cast for *Aïda* fell ill suddenly. Florence Easton vol-
unteered to take her place without rehearsal. Maclennan was the *Rhadames* of the performance. The
Kaiser was present.

He sent for Miss Easton to come to his box between the acts. After offering congratulations, he
anticipated the opera's ending by saying, "It must
be a pleasure for you to die with your husband."

"Yes, Your Majesty, when I can die singing with
him," was her prompt retort.

"Would you like to sing at my opera house?"
the Kaiser asked, his eyes twinkling.

When she regained her breath sufficiently, Miss
Easton answered, "Yes, sir."

Three days later she received a contract with the
Berlin Royal Opera. A dash of the Kaiser's pen had
opened a new chapter in the Easton-Maclennan
singing romance.

For a long time the pair remained prime favorites
in Berlin, and their linked fame spread. Then the
war broke and swept them forth as people of the
Entente Allies. It was but natural that they should

come to America, and but natural, perhaps, that Miss Easton should again give up all to be with her husband, who was engaged for heroic Wagnerian rôles at the Chicago Opera.

When the United States entered the war, Wagner was exiled from our opera houses. This new turn gave Miss Easton an engagement at the Metropolitan Opera in New York. There, in a range of rôles from *Carmen* to *Isolde* and with mounting artistic success she has remained ever since, while Maclennan just as cheerfully as did she for years has sacrificed all to be with her.

Perhaps the romance of the pair is unending. Some day people may be leaving visiting cards on their single tomb, one cannot imagine Florence Easton and Francis Maclennan as having separate ones, and just as they do on the tomb ascribed to Juliet at Verona. For love is the greatest thing in the world; when it lasts throughout life it becomes immortal.

END